Mani Singh Basi is a barrister at 4PB. He is a specialist in family law disputes relating to children, particularly in matters with an international dimension. He regularly appears in complicated cases in the High Court and the Court of Appeal. Mani is an award winning barrister, having won the 2025 LexisNexis International Family Lawyer of the Year award, as well as previously winning the 2024 Legal Personality of the Year award (LexisNexis), the 2024 Legal Aid Barrister of the Year award (Legal Aid Practitioners Group), the 2023 Family Law Junior Barrister of the Year award (LexisNexis) and 2022 Family Law Commentator of the Year award (LexisNexis).

A Practical Guide to Expert Evidence in Proceedings Concerning Children

A Practical Guide to Expert Evidence in Proceedings Concerning Children

Mani Singh Basi

Law Brief Publishing

Published 2026 by Law Brief Publishing, an imprint of Law Brief Publishing Ltd
30 The Parks
Minehead
Somerset
TA24 8BT

www.lawbriefpublishing.com

Paperback: 978-1-918241-15-0

This book is dedicated to my family as well as 4PB for all the support that they have provided me in my career so far. I would also like to thank Emily Otvos, who was my pupil during the time I wrote this book and for all her assistance.

PREFACE

This book provides those with an interest in proceedings concerning children a practical user-friendly guide to help navigate the issue of expert evidence.

The book considers the use of expert evidence across different areas of law including proceedings concerning the 1980 Hague Convention, inherent jurisdiction proceedings, public and private law proceedings. The book focuses on the different type of expert reports, as well as highlighting what practitioners must consider when advising their clients, preparing the application and pursuing it at court. Each chapter also focuses on the benefits of expert evidence and the ability to challenge such evidence where appropriate. The book highlights the relevant rules and law that applies when it comes to expert evidence.

The book is accurate as of 30 November 2025.

Mani Singh Basi
December 2025

CONTENTS

CHAPTER ONE

AN INTRODUCTION TO EXPERT EVIDENCE

Introduction

Expert evidence can be vast and varied when it comes to proceedings concerning children. This book will be focusing on various disciplines within family law where there are some obvious overlaps, but also some key differences. For example, in the international child abduction context, the use, relevance and ultimate purpose of expert evidence can be very different in inherent jurisdiction proceedings to that of 1980 Hague Convention proceedings. Likewise, this book will outline the use of experts in private and public law proceedings and the differences that exist.

Each area of law concerning children can raise different issues, particularly when it comes to welfare. Each area of law also has its own challenges, for example in public law proceedings there is a clear aim to resolve disputes within 26 weeks. In other proceedings, particularly private law proceedings where there are many more litigants in person due to legal aid costs, other challenges exist including costs of experts. Ultimately, expert evidence can be focused on assisting the court with the necessary evidence to timetable and resolve disputes. The different disciplines of experts can also be varied, from independent social workers, to psychiatrists, to risk assessors and legal experts.

It is imperative that practitioners are able to identify the necessity of expert evidence at the earliest possible opportunity. Once the necessity is identified from a lawyer's perspective, it is essential that any application is prepared in the manner to which the rules prescribe. Failure to do so can have consequences. Further, the ability to challenge expert evidence is also a key component to this book.

CHAPTER TWO

EXPERT EVIDENCE: KEY PRINCIPLES

Introduction to the Chapter

This chapter will focus on the key principles when it comes to instruct expert evidence in light of case law but also the Family Procedure Rules 2010 ['FPR']. These key principles are relevant to each area that this book will consider.

Opinion Evidence

Before focusing on expert evidence, the concept of *opinion evidence* will be addressed as it is important from the outset that this is distinguished. Section 3 of the Civil Evidence Act 1972 provides as follows:

> *"3 Admissibility of expert opinion and certain expressions of non-expert opinion*
>
> (1) *Subject to any rules of court made in pursuance of . . . this Act, where a person is called as a witness in any civil proceedings, his opinion on any relevant matter on which he is qualified to give expert evidence shall be admissible in evidence.*
>
> (2) *It is hereby declared that where a person is called as a witness in any civil proceedings, a statement of opinion by him on any relevant matter on which he is not qualified to give expert evidence, if made as a way of conveying relevant facts personally perceived by him, is admissible as evidence of what he perceived.*
>
> (3) *In this section "relevant matter" includes an issue in the proceedings in question."*

> *This provision is extended to include the evidence of a witness who is not called by s.1 of the Civil Evidence Act 1995, which provides:*
>
> "(1) *In civil proceedings evidence shall not be excluded on the ground that it is hearsay.*
>
> (2) *In this Act—*
>
> (a) *hearsay means a statement made otherwise than by a person while giving oral evidence in the proceedings which is tendered as evidence of the matters stated; and*
>
> (b) *references to hearsay include hearsay of whatever degree."*
>
> *Section 13 of the 1995 Act provides that a "statement" means "any representation of fact or opinion, however made". Accordingly, as set out in Phipson, at [29-03], this provision "covers statements of opinion admissible under the 1972 Act".*

As to the admissibility of such evidence, the issue was considered in the Court of Appeal in C v M[1], it was stated at paragraph 81:

> '*This issue is addressed in some detail in Phipson, at [33-112], as set out in D (A Child) at [72], which I repeat (with some footnotes incorporated):*
>
> *"[33-112] Although in general inadmissible, the opinions or beliefs of witnesses who are not experts are admissible in proof of the matters mentioned below, on grounds of necessity, more direct and positive evidence being often unobtainable. Moreover, it has long been thought, and for civil cases it has now been declared by s.3(2) of the Civil Evidence Act 1972, that*

1 [2023] EWCA Civ 1449

non-expert opinion may be received as evidence of the facts intended to be conveyed by that expression of opinion. Thus there is no blanket rule that a factual witness may not include opinion evidence in his witness statement in civil cases. There are numerous authorities which exemplify that a witness of fact may give opinion evidence which relates to the factual evidence he is giving, particularly if he has relevant experience or knowledge. An example is where the evidence given is to a hypothetical situation as to what would or could have happened [MAD Atelier International BV v Manes [2021] EWHC 1899 (Comm) at [11]]. In Rasool v West Midlands Passenger Transport Board [[1974] 3 All E.R. 638] an account of a witness of a road accident was received notwithstanding the fact that it contained the words "the bus driver was in no way to blame for the accident". The court treated them as admissible although the 1972 Act did not fall to be considered, and the point was not argued [This passage in the 17th edition of Phipson was followed in Lawrence v Kent County Council [2012] EWCA Civ 493, which observed that time and time again one sees references to the opinions of a factual witness in judgments without any suggestion that they are totally irrelevant (at [25])].

The statute purports to declare the law, and it is thought that the position must be the same in criminal cases. This proposition is given emphatic support by R. v Johnson [[1994] Crim. L.R. 376 CA] where a witness testified that she had seen the victim of a rape and buggery of the defendant shortly after the incident and that although she had initially thought that the victim was play-acting, she had come to believe that her distress was genuine.

In civil cases, hearsay evidence of opinion is admissible under s.1 of the Civil Evidence Act 1995 (which renders all hearsay,

> *whether of fact or opinion admissible). This provision extends to admissible non expert opinion of the kind discussed here."*
>
> *I do not propose to quote again from Lawrence v Kent County Council [2012] EWCA Civ 493, which is set out in D (A Child), at [73].'*

Expert Evidence – Basic Principles

The key provision is Part 25 of the FPR 2010. Part 25 establishes the procedural framework governing the instruction, use, and control of expert evidence within family proceedings. Its primary purpose is to ensure that expert evidence is used only when necessary and that such evidence assists the court in the resolution of disputes. The rules cement both the overriding duty of experts to the court and the procedural mechanisms for obtaining permission to adduce expert evidence.

The rules contain the following. **25.2** outlines key definitions, including that of proceedings concerning children. **25.2** provides key definitions that shape the operation of Part 25. The term *'children proceedings'* encompasses those referred to in rules **12.1** and **14.1**, as well as any proceedings relating wholly or mainly to the maintenance or upbringing of a minor (**r.25.2(1)(a)**). It also extends to applications for permission to commence or intervene in such proceedings (r.**25.2(1)(b)**–(**c**)). The definition is expressly prescribed for the purposes of section 13(9) of the Children and Families Act 2014.

Part 25 requires reading in full. It includes rules relating to:

Title	Number
Interpretation	Rule 25.2
Experts' overriding duty to the court	Rule 25.3
Control of expert evidence in proceedings other than children proceedings	Rule 25.4
Further provisions about the court's power to restrict expert evidence	Rule 25.5
When to apply for the court's permission	Rule 25.6
What an application notice requesting the court's permission must include	Rule 25.7
Where permission is granted	Rule 25.8
General requirement for expert evidence to be given in a written report	Rule 25.9
Written questions to experts	Rule 25.10
Court's power to direct that evidence is to be given by a single joint expert	Rule 25.11
Instructions to a single joint expert	Rule 25.12
Power of court to direct a party to provide information	Rule 25.13
Contents of report	Rule 25.14

Title	Number
Use by one party of expert's report disclosed by another	Rule 25.15
Discussions between experts	Rule 25.16
Expert's right to ask court for directions	Rule 25.17
Copies of orders and other documents	Rule 25.18
Action after final hearing	Rule 25.19
Assessors	Rule 25.20

The rule also defines *'expert'* as any individual providing expert evidence for use in proceedings, excluding activities that do not constitute expert evidence within the meaning of section 13(8) of the 2014 Act. As outlined by Cazalet J in Note Re R (A Minor) (Expert's Evidence)[2]:

> *'Expert witnesses are in a privileged position; indeed, only experts are permitted to give an opinion in evidence. Outside the legal field the court itself has no expertise and for that reason frequently has to rely on the evidence of experts. Such experts must express only opinions which they genuinely hold and which are not biased in favour of one particular party.'*

A *'single joint expert'* refers to a person instructed jointly by two or more parties (**r.25.2(1)**). The rules deal with a number of key principles, when it comes to preparing

2 [1991] 1 FLR 291

applications, asking questions of the expert, and the duties of experts.

Duties of Experts

Rule **25.3** establishes that experts owe their paramount duty to the court rather than to the party instructing or remunerating them. This duty of independence and impartiality is reinforced by Practice Direction 25B, which delineates the particular responsibilities of experts, including the contents and form of their reports, and their obligation to attend court where necessary.

Control of Expert Evidence

For proceedings concerning children, the control of expert evidence is governed by section 13 of the Children and Families Act 2014, which imposes a similarly stringent test of necessity and underscores judicial control over expert involvement.

Sir James Munby P of *Re: H L (A Child)* [3] defined "necessary" as:

> *'Lying somewhere between 'indispensable' on the one hand and 'useful', 'reasonable' or 'desirable' on the other hand', having "the connotation of the imperative, what is demanded rather than what is merely optional or reasonable or desirable'.*

Further, Sir James Munby P in Re H-L (Expert Evidence: Test for Permission)[4]: stated:

> *'[3] … is that "necessary" means necessary. It is, after all, an ordinary English word. It is a familiar expression nowadays in family law, not least because of the central role it plays, for*

3 [2013] EWCA Civ 655

4 [2013] EWCA 655

> *example, in Article 8 of the European Convention and the wider Strasbourg jurisprudence ... It "has a meaning lying somewhere between 'indispensable' on the one hand and 'useful', 'reasonable' or 'desirable' on the other hand", having "the connotation of the imperative, what is demanded rather than what is merely optional or reasonable or desirable."'"*

Section 13(7) of the CFA 2014 sets out the factors to be considered by the court when deciding whether to give permission

Factors relevant to the court

Rule **25.5** outlines the considerations the court must consider when determining whether to grant permission. In children proceedings, the court must consider compliance with rule 25.6 and any previous directions concerning expert evidence (**r.25.5(1)**). This is treated as a prescribed matter under section 13(7)(h) of the Children and Families Act 2014 and section 38(7B) of the Children Act 1989 *(r.25.5(1A))*

Timing and Contents of the Application

Parties are required to apply for permission to instruct experts as soon as possible (**r.25.6**). Specific deadlines are provided depending on the nature of the proceedings—for instance, by the Case Management Hearing in public law cases, or by the First Hearing Dispute Resolution Appointment in private law cases (**r.25.6(a)–(e)**).

Under rule **25.7**, applications must comply with Part 18 and include the expert's field, name (if known), relevant issues, consideration of a single joint expert, and other matters specified in Practice Directions 25C *or* 25D. In children proceedings, the application will also specify the questions for the expert to answer (**r.25.7(3)**)

Expert Report and Questions

Expert evidence is generally to be given in writing (**r.25.9(1)**), and attendance at hearings will only be required when necessary for justice (**r.25.9(2)**).

Parties may put written *questions* to experts for clarification purposes (**r.25.10(1)**), but such questions must be proportionate, limited to one occasion, and submitted within ten days of receiving the report (**r.25.10(2)**). Non-compliance by an expert may lead to sanctions against the instructing party, including exclusion of the evidence or disallowance of expert costs (**r.25.10(4)**)

Single Joint Experts

The court may direct that expert evidence be provided by a single joint expert where two or more parties wish to adduce evidence on the same issue (r.**25.11**(1)). If the parties cannot agree on the expert, the court may select one from a proposed list or determine another method of selection (**r.25.11(2)**). In practice, when parties are legally represented it is good practice to highlight and inform the other side of an intention to prepare a part 25 application. This will enable a collaborative approach to be utilised, including agreeing questions on and either / or basis, and identifying experts.

Rule **25.12** regulates instructions to single joint experts, which should ordinarily be set out in a jointly agreed letter. The court may also issue directions on payment, assessments, and fee limits, with parties being jointly and severally liable for payment unless otherwise directed (**r.25.12(6)**). If any party seeks a variation, or different provisions to apply to this, it must be address when making the application.

Other Provisions

An expert's report must comply with Practice Direction 25B and include a declaration of compliance with the expert's overriding duty (**r.25.14(2)**). Instructions to experts are not privileged (**r.25.14(3)**). Once disclosed, any party may rely on another's expert report at a hearing (**r.25.15**).

The court may direct discussions between experts to identify and narrow issues in dispute, culminating in a statement of agreed and disagreed points with reasons (**r.25.16**). This promotes efficiency and reduces duplication of expert opinion.

Costs and Legal Aid

There can sometimes be issues relating to costs of experts. For example, if one party is legally aided and the other is not, or if the expert does not work within legal aid rates. These unfortunate issues can cause a delay to the proceedings. The costs of an expert is a consideration for the court (r.**25.5** (e)).

Where the costs of the expert are going to be paid by one party alone, for example on their legal aid certificate, the judge should do a financial assessment and outline this on the face of the order as to why the other party should not share any costs. Where legal aid exists, there can be different approaches to be adopted. For example, a party may need to apply for 'prior authority' if the fees / expert hours are outside the usual scope for the legal aid certificate.

In international child abduction disputes, there are occasions when the issue as to the costs are dealt with at the end of the proceedings. An example of this arises from a specific judgment considering the costs of expert report as well as translation costs in MB v KB & Ors (Costs)[5].

Conclusion of Chapter

Part 25 of the Family Procedure Rules 2010 codifies a rigorous framework for the management of expert evidence, balancing the necessity for specialist input against the imperatives of proportionality, cost-efficiency, and judicial control. Its provisions reinforce the expert's independence, promote cooperation between parties, and underscore the court's ultimate authority in determining the scope and admissibility of expert evidence. Collectively, these rules require consideration alongside overriding objective of the FPR and practitioners should think about expert evidence in a manner which will enable cases to be dealt with justly, efficiently, and with due regard to the welfare of children. However, each case and area of law is fact specific and as such different considerations can arise.

Practitioners should also not forget reference the Children and Families Act 2014. Further, the manner in which expert evidence can be challenged and the strategic reason for doing so is again, fact specific and will be considered in each of the specialist chapters in this book. Practitioners should also consider the draft orders / precedents that exist, either prepared by Mr Justice Peel or whatever the local court utilise. These orders often include the necessary wording when it comes to the preparation of Part 25's, granting of the applications and other provisions concerning experts, such as costs, further questions and attendance at hearings.

5 [2023] EWHC 3299 (Fam)

CHAPTER THREE

EXPERT EVIDENCE IN 1980 HAGUE CONVENTION PROCEEDINGS

1980 Hague Convention Proceedings – Underlying Principles

To fully understand the role of expert evidence in 1980 Hague Convention proceedings, the issues that such proceedings are designed to grapple with requires to be set out.

This Convention has a number of signatories, approximately close to 100 countries. The Convention sets out clearly in Article 1 a clear aim: *'The objects of the present Convention are -*

> *a) to secure the prompt return of children wrongfully removed to or retained in any Contracting State; and*
>
> *b) to ensure that rights of custody and of access under the law of one Contracting State are effectively respected in the other Contracting States'*

Further, Article 2 and 11 sets out the need for proceedings under the 1980 Hague Convention to be dealt with expeditiously. Article 2 states:

> *'Contracting States shall take all appropriate measures to secure within their territories the implementation of the objects of the Convention. For this purpose they shall use the most expeditious procedures available'*

Article 11 states:

'The judicial or administrative authorities of Contracting States shall act expeditiously in proceedings for the return of children.

If the judicial or administrative authority concerned has not reached a decision within six weeks from the date of commencement of the proceedings, the applicant or the Central Authority of the requested State, on its own initiative or if asked by the Central Authority of the requesting State, shall have the right to request a statement of the reasons for the delay. If a reply is received by the Central Authority of the requested State, that Authority shall transmit the reply to the Central Authority of the requesting State, or to the applicant, as the case may be'.

It is therefore apparent from its language; the Convention is a strict treaty with focused aims. It outlined the impact upon child abduction and how states who are signatories to the Convention must act expeditiously in determining a 1980 Hague Convention.

In England, 1980 Hague Convention cases are heard in the High Court also. For example, if a child is abducted from a signatory to the Convention to this country, the proceedings will commence in the High Court and remain there until the conclusion of the proceedings. High Court judges are therefore particularly experienced at dealing with child abduction matters. The provisions are often regarded as being interpreted narrowly because the aim is to return children to the country of their habitual residence. The Convention considers in detail what is regarded as wrongful removal or wrongful retention and what the exceptions to a summary return are. Perhaps the matter can be explained nicely by Mostyn J in B v B[6] where his lordship stated:

'2 The Hague Convention of 1980 is arguably the most successful ever international treaty and it has over 90 subscribers to it, over half the countries in the world. The underlying and

6 [2014] EWHC 1804

central foundation of the Convention is that, where a child has been unilaterally removed from the land of her habitual residence in breach of someone's rights of custody, then she should be swiftly returned to that country for the courts of that country to decide on her long-term future.

3 There are very few exceptions to this and the exceptions that do exist have to be interpreted very narrowly in order that the central premise of the Convention is not fatally undermined. It is important to understand what the Convention does not do. The Convention does not order a child who has been removed in the circumstances I have described to live with anybody. The Convention does not provide that the parent who is left behind should, on the return of the child, have contact or access in any particular way. The Convention does not provide that, when an order for return to the child's homeland is made, the child should stay there indefinitely. All the Convention provides is that the child should be returned for the specific purpose and limited period to enable the court of her homeland to decide on her long-term future. That is all it decides.

4 ... Equally, if the exception that is relied on is that there is a grave risk that his or her return would expose the child to physical or psychological harm or otherwise place her in an intolerable situation, that again has to be seen through the lens of the objective of the Convention. We are not talking here about long- term risks. We are not talking here about long-term harm. We are talking about risks and harm that would eventuate only in the period that it takes for the court of the child's homeland to determine her long-term future and to impose the necessary safeguards, if necessary, in the interim.'

Further in Re D (A Child) (Abduction: Rights of Custody)[7], Baroness Hale of Richmond observed:

> *'The whole object of the Convention is to secure the swift return of children wrongfully removed from their home country, not only so that they can return to the place which is properly their 'home', but also so that any dispute about where they should live in the future can be decided in the courts of their home country, according to the laws of their home country and in accordance with the evidence which will mostly be there rather than in the country to which they have been removed'*

The Exceptions to a Return

In 1980 Hague Convention defences, a party may raise a defence / exception to the principles relating to a return. This must be considered at the first on-notice hearing, because it is fundamental to timetabling the proceedings. As such, in addition to expert evidence, concepts such as Cafcass involvement requires consideration.

In short, there are a number of avenues that a respondent may raise to defend a 1980 Hague Convention case. These can encompass:

- Rights of custody;
- Habitual residence;
- Consent / acquiescence;
- Article 13(b);
- Child objections;

[7] [2006] UKLH 51, para 48

- Settlement.

Applicants may also seek to take the lead in obtaining expert evidence, particularly when it comes to issues relating to protective measures and rights of custody. Expert evidence often falls under the Article 13(b) category and can also appear in cases where there are issues relating to 'rights of custody'.

<u>Article 13(b) grave risk of harm / intolerability</u>

The wording of Article 13b needs to be considered in full. The leading authority is that of Re E[8] and since then there has been a significant amount of appellant authorities. A useful summary arises in Re A (Article 13(b): (Mental Ill-health))[9]. It was stated:

> *'The following principles emerge from these authorities, relevant to the 1980 Hague application:*
>
> *i) Article 13(b) is, by its very terms, of restricted application: [§31: Re E (Children)]; the defence has a high threshold;*
>
> *ii) The focus must be on the child, and the risk to the child in the event of a return;*
>
> *iii) The burden of proof lies with the person, institution or other body which opposes the child's return. The standard of proof is the ordinary balance of probabilities, subject to the summary nature of the Hague Convention process: [§32: Re E (Children)];*

---

8 [2011] UKSC 27

9 [2023] EWHC 2082 (Fam).

iv) The risk to the child must be "grave" and, although that characterises the risk rather than the harm, "there is in ordinary language a link between the two": [§33: Re E (Children)];

v) "Intolerable" is a strong word, but when applied to a child must mean a situation which this particular child in these particular circumstances should not be expected to tolerate. Amongst these are physical or psychological abuse or neglect of the child: [§34: Re E (Children)];

vi) Article 13(b) is looking to the future, namely the situation as it would be if the child were to be returned forthwith to his home country: [§35: Re E (Children)];

vii) In a case where allegations of domestic abuse are made:

> *"... the court should first ask whether, if they are true, there would be a grave risk that the child would be exposed to physical or psychological harm or otherwise placed in an intolerable situation. If so, the court must then ask how the child can be protected against the risk. The appropriate protective measures and their efficacy will obviously vary from case to case and from country to country. This is where arrangements for international co-operation between liaison Judges are so helpful." [§36]: Re E (Children) (Emphasis by italics added).*

viii) In this case, the passage in §34 of Re S (Lord Wilson) ...:

> *"The critical question is what will happen if, with the mother, the child is returned. If the court concludes that, on return, <u>the mother will suffer such anxieties that their effect on her mental health will create a situation that is intolerable for the child, then the child should not be returned.</u> It matters not whether the mother's anxieties will be reasonable or unreasonable. The extent to which there will, objectively, be*

> *good cause for the mother to be anxious on return will nevertheless be relevant to the court's assessment of the mother's mental state if the child is returned".*

ix) The court must examine in concrete terms the situation in which the child would be on a return. In analysing whether the allegations are of sufficient detail and substance to give rise to the grave risk, the judge will have to consider whether the evidence enables him or her confidently to discount the possibility that they do;

x) The situation which the child will face on return depends crucially on the protective measures which can be put in place to ensure that the child will not be called upon to face an intolerable situation when he or she gets home. Thus:

> *"... the clearer the need for protection, the more effective the measures will have to be" [§52: Re E (Children)]*

35. Moylan LJ in Re C [2021] (citation above) emphasised that the risk to the child must be a future risk (§49-50). He cited from the Good Practice Guide to emphasise that:

> *"... forward-looking does not mean that past behaviours and incidents cannot be relevant to the assessment of a grave risk upon the return of the child to the State of habitual residence. For example, past incidents of domestic or family violence may, depending on the particular circumstances, be probative on the issue of whether such a grave risk exists. That said, past behaviours and incidents are not per se determinative of the fact that effective protective measures are not available to protect the child from the grave risk". (§50)*

36. Thus, an assessment needs to be made of the

> *"... circumstances as they would be if the child were to be returned forthwith. The examination of the grave risk exception should then also include, if considered necessary and appropriate, consideration of the availability of adequate and effective measures of protection in the State of habitual residence" (§50).*

He added:

> *"It is also axiomatic that the risk arising from the child's return must be grave. Again quoting from Re E, at [33]: "It must have reached such a level of seriousness as to be characterised as 'grave'". As set out in Re A, at [99], this requires an analysis "of the nature and degree of the risk(s)" in order to determine whether the required grave risk is established" (emphasis in the original).*

37. *I am clear that my role is not to engage in a fact-finding exercise, but as Moylan LJ went on to observe:*

38. *"... unless the court properly analyses the nature and severity of the potential risk which it is said will arise if the child is returned to the requesting State, the court will not be in a position properly to assess whether the available protective measures will sufficiently address or ameliorate that risk such that the grave risk required by Article 13(b) will not have been established. As set out in Re E, at [36], the question the court is considering is "how the child can be protected against the risk" (my emphasis). The whole analysis is contextual and forms part of the court's process of reasoning, as referred to by me in Re A, at [97], adopting this expression from Re S (A Child) (Abduction: Rights of Custody) [2012] 2 AC 257, at [22]". (§58)In his judgment, Moylan LJ took the opportunity to emphasise the importance of adherence to Practice Guidance: Case Management and Mediation of International Child Abduction Proceedings issued by Sir James Munby P on 13*

March 2018, and to the point that protective measures include not only those offered by the left-behind parent but also those available ordinarily in the state of habitual residence and their adequacy and effectiveness (§60).

39. *I also have regard, as I must to the definition of domestic abuse contained in section 1(3) of the Domestic Abuse Act 2021 and PD12J FPR 2010,*

40. *It is relevant, in a case in which the mother has raised both domestic abuse and mental health issues, that I look at the allegations cumulatively and not independent of each other. In re B (Children) [2022] 3 WLR 1315, Moylan LJ said:*

> *"[70] The authorities make clear that the court is evaluating whether there is a grave risk based on the allegations relied on by the taking parent as a whole, not individually. There may, of course, be distinct strands which have to be analysed separately but the court must not overlook the need to consider the cumulative effect of those allegations for the purpose of evaluating the nature and level of any grave risk(s) that might potentially be established as well as the protective measures available to address such risk(s)." (emphasis by underlining added).'*

The first assessment is whether the threshold has been crossed.

Crossing the threshold

In Re E the Supreme Court reiterated the test to be applied when assessing an article 13(b) defence at [**31** – **35**]:

> '[**31**] *Both Professor Pérez-Vera and the House of Lords referred to the application, rather than the interpretation, of Art 13. We share the view expressed in the High Court of Australia in DP v Commonwealth Central Authority; JLM v Director-General*

NSW Department of Community Services [2001] HCA 39, paras 9, 44, that there is no need for the Article to be 'narrowly construed'. By its very terms, it is of restricted application. The words of Art 13 are quite plain and need no further elaboration or 'gloss'.

[32] *First, it is clear that the burden of proof lies with the 'person, institution or other body' which opposes the child's return. It is for them to produce evidence to substantiate one of the exceptions. There is nothing to indicate that the standard of proof is other than the ordinary balance of probabilities. But in evaluating the evidence the court will, of course, be mindful of the limitations involved in the summary nature of the Hague Convention process. It will rarely be appropriate to hear oral evidence of the allegations made under Art 13(b) and so neither those allegations nor their rebuttal are usually tested in cross-examination.*

[33] *Second, the risk to the child must be 'grave'. It is not enough, as it is in other contexts such as asylum, that the risk be 'real'. It must have reached such a level of seriousness as to be characterised as 'grave'. Although 'grave' characterises the risk rather than the harm, there is in ordinary language a link between the two. Thus a relatively low risk of death or really serious injury might properly be qualified as 'grave' while a higher level of risk might be required for other less serious forms of harm.*

[34] *Third, the words 'physical or psychological harm' are not qualified. However, they do gain colour from the alternative 'or otherwise' placed 'in an intolerable situation' (emphasis supplied). As was said in Re D, at para [52], '"Intolerable" is a strong word, but when applied to a child must mean "a situation which this particular child in these particular circumstances should not be expected to tolerate"'. Those words were carefully*

considered and can be applied just as sensibly to physical or psychological harm as to any other situation. Every child has to put up with a certain amount of rough and tumble, discomfort and distress. It is part of growing up. But there are some things which it is not reasonable to expect a child to tolerate. Among these, of course, are physical or psychological abuse or neglect of the child herself. Among these also, we now understand, can be exposure to the harmful effects of seeing and hearing the physical or psychological abuse of her own parent. Mr Turner accepts that, if there is such a risk, the source of it is irrelevant: eg, where a mother's subjective perception of events leads to a mental illness which could have intolerable consequences for the child.

Once the threshold is crossed – assessing protective measures

39. In Re E, the Supreme Court made the following points in respect of protective measures:

'[35] Fourth, Art 13(b) is looking to the future: the situation as it would be if the child were to be returned forthwith to her home country. As has often been pointed out, this is not necessarily the same as being returned to the person, institution or other body who has requested her return, although, of course, it may be so if that person has the right so to demand. More importantly, the situation which the child will face on return depends crucially on the protective measures which can be put in place to secure that the child will not be called upon to face an intolerable situation when she gets home. Mr Turner accepts that if the risk is serious enough to fall within Art 13(b) the court is not only concerned with the child's immediate future, because the need for effective protection may persist.

[36] There is obviously a tension between the inability of the court to resolve factual disputes between the parties and the risks that the child will face if the allegations are in fact true. Mr Turner submits that there is a sensible and pragmatic solution.

Where allegations of domestic abuse are made, the court should first ask whether, if they are true, there would be a grave risk that the child would be exposed to physical or psychological harm or otherwise placed in an intolerable situation. If so, the court must then ask how the child can be protected against the risk. The appropriate protective measures and their efficacy will obviously vary from case to case and from country to country. This is where arrangements for international co-operation between liaison judges are so helpful. Without such protective measures, the court may have no option but to do the best it can to resolve the disputed issues.

[37] To this Mr Setright would add that it would be even more helpful if there were machinery in place for recognising and enforcing protective orders (and, between common law countries at least, undertakings given to the courts) made in the Requested State in order to protect the children on their return to the Requesting State at least until the courts of the Requesting State are seised of the case (if they ever are). The Brussels II revised Regulation clearly contemplates that adequate measures actually be in force and without some such machinery this may not always be possible. We, therefore, take this opportunity to urge the Hague Conference to consider whether machinery can be put in place whereby, when the courts of the Requested State identify specific protective measures as necessary if the Art 13(b) exception is to be rejected, then those measures can become enforceable in the Requesting State, for a temporary period at least, before the child is returned.'

Now that the scene is set, there are in short two key considerations when it comes to Article 13(b). The first is the risk, i.e what does it relate to, and secondly that of protective measures. Expert evidence can fall under both strands.

Article 13b – Expert Evidence

Respondents may seek to advance a case under Article 13b which will require the need for expert evidence. Typically, this can be formed in many different ways, and each case is of course fact-specific. However, there are a number of common threads in 1980 Hague Convention which are:

- Mental Health; and

- Protective Measures.

There are also other issues that can arise, such as risk of prosecution and also immigration issues.

Mental Health

The respondent may seek to make an application for a psychological / psychiatric report in 1980 Hague Convention proceedings. The starting point is S (A Child)[10], where the Supreme Court made clear at (at paragraph 27) that the subjective anxieties of a respondent can found an article 13(b) defence. Further, the Supreme Court stated that the decision of the court in Re E was not a *'restatement' of the law of the Convention: it was primarily an exercise in the removal from it of disfiguring excrescence'* (at paragraph 31).

There is a number of first instant decisions focusing on the issue of mental health, such as Re A (Article 13(b)): Mental Ill-Health)[11], Re

---

10 [2012] UKSC 10

11 [2023] EWHC 2082 (Fam)

K & S (Article 13(b)[12], K v E[13], M (A Child) (1980 Hague Convention: Abduction: Article 13(b) Mental Health)[14] and D v E[15].

As such, a respondent may seek to make an application pursuant to the Part25 process. This relates to Article 13b, and such applications go to the heart of the following arguments arising from Re E:

The burden of proof in establishing 'grave risk' opposing the return [Re E at §32];

- The risk must be 'grave'. A relatively low risk of death might properly be qualified as grave; whilst a higher level or risk might be required for other (less serious) forms of harm [Re E at §33];

- 'Physical or psychological harm' and 'intolerable situation' are not defined but when applied are child and situation specific, i.e. the situation which these children in their circumstances should not be expected to tolerate. That does not mean some rough and tumble; but that which is not reasonable to expect a child to tolerate [Re E at §34];

- Article 13(b) looks to the future and the situation on return. It depends 'crucially' on the protective measures that can be put in place [Re E at §35];

- If the risks are serious enough to fall within article 13(b), the Court is not only concerned with the child's immediate future,

12 [2023] EWHC 1883 (Fam)

13 [2023] EWHC 2890 (Fam)

14 [2023] EWHC 3164 (Fam)

15 [2025] EWHC 1172 (Fam)

because the need for effective protection may persist [Re E at §35].

Accordingly, a respondent's mental health can be a tricky issue, when looking ahead and at the future. An expert will be required to make that assessment, and the judge will be required as part of the final hearing to consider the threshold and whether protective measures can ameliorate any impact, including any deterioration in mental health. The key question has recently been clarified in the Court of Appeal, by Moylan LJ at paragraph 54 in Re B (Abduction: Article 13(b): Mental Health)[16]:

> *'the key question, not in abstract but in real terms and adopting what Lord Wilson said in Re S, is what is likely to happen if the mother and A were to return to Australia. Is the likely effect on the mother's mental health sufficient to establish a grave risk that A would be exposed to physical or psychological harm or otherwise placed in an intolerable situation? As referred to above, this requires consideration of the nature of the risk; the likelihood of the risk materialising; and the consequences of the risk materialising for A. These are for the purposes of answering the ultimate question, namely whether there is a grave risk that returning A to Australia would expose her to psychological harm or otherwise place her in an intolerable situation'.*

Further at paragraph 59:

> *'I would first note that Dr Ratnam's evidence was that there is a significant risk of deterioration and not a risk of significant deterioration. This is not a semantic distinction but an important substantive distinction. I would, for example, refer again to Re S in which the expert said, at [25]: "the likely psychiatric and psychological impact on [the mother] of a return*

[16] [2024] EWHA Civ 1595

to Australia is significant and severe" and In re B (A Child) [2021] 1 WLR 517 in which, at [111], "Dr Ratnam's evidence ... established that the mother's mental health would be likely significantly to deteriorate" on a return to Bosnia. Dr Ratnam's evidence, that there was a significant risk, does not, therefore, support the judge's conclusions that there was a risk of, what would clearly be, a very significant deterioration. I would also reject Mr Gupta's submission that when Dr Ratnam said that there was a "significant" risk of deterioration this Judgment Approved by the court for handing down. B (A Child) "can be equated with 'grave'". Her evidence was directed to the level of the risk not the nature of the deterioration'

Practice Points – Mental Health

It is imperative those representing the respondent are alive to the issues at the first on-notice hearing. A history of the respondent's current circumstances and history relating to mental health should be taken. If a party is not in a position to make a formal part25 application, the issue should be flagged up at the first hearing and a specific date recorded in the order encompassing any anticipated application. Due to the requirements of Article 11 of 1980 Hague Convention, proceedings are timetabled in a strict manner. It is essential any expert evidence can report within court timescales.

A part 25 application has to be full. The letter of instruction should be available at the hearing, to enable the court to consider the questions the expert is due to be asked.

For applicants, likewise they need to be full and frank at the outset about whether it is anticipated a respondent is likely to raise mental health issues. If so, this can be anticipated and accounted for in the court timetable. When it comes to protective measures, it is imperative an applicant is able to address the issue, whether it is therapeutic, medical insurance or any other mental health services that may be available in the left behind state.

Protective Measures – Legal Experts

As outlined above when considering Article 13b, a key consideration for the court is the issues of protective measures. The Court of Appeal has given guidance as regards the need for the Hague court to carefully scrutinise and consider the efficacy of protective measures.

In Re C (Children) (Abduction: Article 13(b))[17], Moylan LJ stated at paragraphs 40 – 45:

> *'[40] As was made clear in Re S (A Child) (Abduction: Rights of Custody) [2012] UKSC 10, [2012] 2 AC 257, [2012] 2 WLR 721, [2012] 2 FLR 442, at para [22], the approach 'commended in Re E should form part of the court's general process of reasoning in its appraisal of a defence under the Article'. This appraisal is, itself, general in that it has to take into account all relevant matters which can include measures available in the home state which might ameliorate or obviate the matters relied on in support of the defence. As referred to in Re D (A Child) (Abduction: Custody Rights) [2006] UKHL 51, [2007] 1 AC 619, [2006] 3 WLR 989, [2007] 1 FLR 961, at para [52], the English courts have sought to address the alleged risk by 'extracting undertakings from the applicant as to the conditions in which the child will live when he returns and by relying on the courts of the requesting state to protect him once he is there. In many cases this will be sufficient' (my emphasis).*
>
> *[41] I would also note that the measures being considered are, potentially, anything which might impact on the matters relied upon in support of the Art 13(b) defence and, for example, can include general features of the home State such as access to courts and other State services. The expression 'protective measures' is a broad concept and is not confined to specific measures such as*

17 [2019] 1 FLR 1045

the father proposed in this case. It can include, as I have said, any 'measure' which might address the risk being advanced by the respondent, including 'relying on the courts of the requesting state'. Accordingly, the general right to seek the assistance of the court or other State authorities might in some cases be sufficient to persuade a court that there was not a grave risk within Art 13(b).

[42] In the light of the submissions made in the present case, I would make two further brief observations. They are brief because this is not the occasion for a detailed analysis of the issues.

[43] *First, in respect of Ms Cooper's submissions about the efficacy of undertakings given to the English court, it is clear that, in deciding what weight can be placed on them, the court has to take into account the extent to which they are likely to be effective. This applies both in terms of compliance and in terms of consequences, including remedies, in the absence of compliance. The issue is their effectiveness which is not confined to their enforceability: see, for example, H v K and Others (Abduction: Undertakings)* [2017] EWHC 1141 (Fam), [2018] 1 FLR 700, *at para [61]. In saying this, because I acknowledge the concerns that have been expressed about the court's perhaps giving insufficient weight to the point made by Ms Cooper and the need for caution when relying on undertakings, I make clear that I am not saying that enforceability is not an issue, only that it forms one element of the court's assessment.*

[44] *Secondly, as referred to above, we were told by Mr Jarman that the issue of the enforceability in South Africa of the specific measures proposed in this case, and about which the judge raised doubts (in para [34]), was not raised either before or at the hearing below. From the statements it appeared that the issue was only whether the undertakings should be lodged with the*

court in South Africa or whether an order should be made there. From the submissions, as set out in the judgment (para [34]), it appears that the issue was when the undertakings should be lodged. In any event, if enforceability was to be an issue, it should have been raised well before the hearing.

[45] The President of the Family Division issued Practice Guidance on 13 March 2018: Case Management and Mediation of International Child Abduction Proceedings [2018] Fam Law 448. The issue of protective measures is dealt with in a number of paragraphs which make clear that the issue of specific protective measures, both proposed and sought, must be addressed at the earliest opportunity. It also makes clear that, when required, steps must be taken 'in the most expeditious way available, to ensure that information is obtained, whether from the central authority of the requesting State or otherwise, as to the protective measures that are available, or could be put in place, to meet the alleged identified risks'; para 2.11(e). At para 3.12 reference is made to International Judicial Liaison as being one means of ascertaining whether the courts of the home state 'can accept and enforce orders made or undertakings offered by the parties' in that state or can make a 'mirror order'.

The issue of expert evidence in cases where protective measures is an issue had occurred in the Court of Appeal, Per Moylan LJ in Re T (Abduction: Protective Measures: Agreement to Return)[18]. His lordship stated:

'Protective Measures need to be what they say they are, namely, protective. To be protective, they need to be effective' (at paragraph 50). Borrowing this summary:

18 [2023] EWCA Civ 1415

'Five short points about 'protective measures' merit some consideration within this judgment arising from the appeal:

i) The requirement for the parties to address protective measures early in the process;

ii) The importance of the court identifying early in the proceedings what case management directions need to be made, so that at the final hearing the court has the information necessary to make an informed assessment of the efficacy of protective measures;

iii) The need for the court to be satisfied, when necessary for the purposes of determining whether to make a summary return order, that the proposed protective measures are going to be sufficiently effective in the requesting state to address the article 13(b) risks;

iv) The status of undertakings containing protective measures, and their recognition in foreign states;

v) The distinction between 'protective measures' and 'soft landing' or 'safe harbour' provisions.'

Expert Evidence – Protective Measures – In Practice

Re T raised a number of important points, which requires full reading alongside the Presidents Guidance of March 2023. In short, 1980 Hague Convention proceedings can raise a number of issues relating to:

- The status of undertakings;
- Recognition of undertakings / orders in the left behind state;
- The difference between protective measures and soft landing provisions; and

- The role of 1996 Hague Convention.

Each case is fact-specific and depends on the case the respondent is raising. Again, this should be flagged at the first inter partes hearing. A full part25 application is necessary, alongside the questions. A useful first instance decision on the use of expert evidence on the issue of protective measures can be found in G v K[19].

Expert Evidence – Legal Systems

The case of LM v DR[20] demonstrates the issue that sometimes there can be a challenge to a legal system a country operates. This can relate to a number of different issues. For example, a respondent may allege protective is not available in another country, or benefits aren't available etc, all going towards the issue of Article 13b. The use of experts in this manner is similar to the issue of protective measures, but sometimes a respondent can directly be challenging the protection available in another country. However, in AT v SS[21], MacDonald J commented:

> '62. *In this regard, I must assume (the contrary not having been proved) that the administrative, judicial and social services in Holland are as adept at protecting S as the administrative, judicial and social services in this jurisdiction. In particular, I must assume that Holland has adequate procedures for protecting S in foster care, which procedures extend to ensuring that any psychological distress consequent upon his temporary separation from his primary carer is appropriately addressed (Re S (Abduction: Return to Care) [1999] 1 FLR 843).*

19 [2025] EWHC 2961 (Fam)

20 [2016] EWHC 1943 (Fam)

21 [2015] EWHC 2703 [Fam)

> *64. It would also in my judgment be wrong in this case to allow the mother to frustrate the aims of the Convention by relying on a situation which she herself has brought about. However, whilst it is vitally important that the court maintains fidelity to the principles and aims of the 1980 Convention, I make clear that the driving factor in my decision that in this case the defence under Art 13(b) is not made out is my conclusion that the level of distress and upset that will be caused to S by separation from his mother and placement in foster care in Holland does not meet the criteria for establishing that defence'.*

Therefore, a respondent will have the burden to provide evidence to justify their case. They will have to make such a part25 application.

Criminal Complaint

Other issues can also arise, again perhaps linked with protective measures. For example, issues can arise about risk of prosecution if a respondent who is the primary carer is likely to be prosecuted due to an allegation of child abduction and the respondent is perhaps the primary carer of the children. Expert evidence on the criminal issues is likely to be relevant. In practice, an applicant would normally give an undertaking not to pursue any civil / criminal charge, but it may be apparent that they have already started the process or made a police complaint. Therefore, it is important this issue is flagged by applicant and respondents at the first available opportunity.

In terms of general guidance on this issue, Macdonald J outlined the approach to be taken where a respondent seeks to argue that an Article 13b defence can be founded upon the risk of criminal prosecution arising from the fact they can be charged with the offence of child abduction. In Uhd v McKay (Abduction: Publicity)[22], the judge said as follows:

---

[22] [2019] 2 FLR 1159

'[88] Generally, the risk of the abducting parent being arrested and prosecuted for child abduction is not sufficient by itself to satisfy Art 13(b). In Re L (Abduction: Pending Criminal Proceedings) [1999] 1 FLR 433, the possibility of criminal proceedings being brought and even the possibility of the mother being arrested at the airport on her return was not enough to establish a grave risk of harm to the children. In Re C (Abduction: Grave Risk of Psychological Harm) [1999] 1 FLR 1145, the possibility that the father would change his mind and bring criminal proceedings against the mother if she returned to the USA was likewise not sufficient to establish the exception under Art 13(b). Within this context, in H v K and Others (Abduction: Undertakings) [2017] EWHC 1141 (Fam), [2018] 1 FLR 700, at paras [55]–[57] I observed as follows in respect of the risk of arrest and prosecution:

'(55) With respect to the mother's submission that the children will be placed in an intolerable situation if she is arrested and prosecuted for child abduction, in that this will deprive them of their primary carer, I accept that this risk cannot be entirely ruled out in this case given the understandable reticence of the FBI to reveal details of the existence or progress of any federal investigation. Indeed, in almost all cases it will not be possible to exclude entirely the risk that the abducting parent will face arrest and prosecution on return. The authorities make clear that this risk will generally not be sufficient to satisfy the terms of Art 13(b) of the 1980 Hague Convention.

(56) Two further points fall to be made in this regard. First, a parent who chooses to abduct a child from one jurisdiction to another must expect to be the subject of arrest and prosecution. That is simply one of the proper consequences of a parent unwisely taking the law into his or her own hands rather than seeking relief through the courts. It sits ill in the mouth of a parent who has abducted a child to complain about the

consequent risk of arrest and prosecution. Within this context, there is a principled argument that the court seeking to enforce the return of the child, and thereby maintain fidelity to an international instrument designed to discourage and prevent child abduction, has no business trying to protect the abducting parent from arrest and prosecution upon their return under domestic laws designed to achieve precisely the same end.

[57] Secondly, and within this context, I am unable to accept Mr Devereux's submission that the caveats that the father seeks to add to his undertaking not to support criminal proceedings against the mother with respect to her abduction of the children from the jurisdiction of the US, namely that he will so undertake "to the extent that this does not violate or breach any public policy, statute, regulation, court order or other legal duty on the father" are inappropriate or devalue the undertaking. In my judgment, it is perfectly proper for the father to ensure that his undertaking does not bring him into conflict with the domestic laws of the US. Once again, there is a principled argument that it would be entirely wrong to expect the innocent left behind parent to place themselves in conflict with the laws of their home country in order to prevent the lawful arrest and prosecution of the culpable abducting parent. In short, it is wrong in principle to expect the left behind parent to assume some of the legal risk created by the abducting parent by giving undertakings that have the potential to, or do come into conflict with the laws of the home state. In the circumstances, I am satisfied that the caveats the father places on his undertaking are both reasonable and necessary.'

[89] In the context of this case, the court must also have regard when considering the risk to Ruby of her mother being arrested and detained, to the fact that the Australian Family Court was sufficiently confident in the assessments of the father to order that upon her return, Ruby be placed in his custody, notwithstanding

the allegations made by the mother. In this latter context, whilst an undoubtedly disturbing prospect for the mother, the fact that the mother may be liable to arrest and, following a trial, to imprisonment for child abduction is less likely to represent a grave risk of exposure to harm ....'

Immigration

There can also be other barriers in existence, relating to the immigration status of the respondent and / or children upon a return back. Again, specific and niche expert evidence on this issue will likely be required. A useful example of this arising in recent times can be found in YM v ML[23]. There are also a number of other decisions raising this, such as:

- Re W (Abduction: Intolerable Situation)[24];
- H v O and D, Y and B and Secretary of State for the Home Department[25];
- HZ v GA[26]; and
- K v M[27]

In making an application, extracts from Moylan LJ in *Re B (Children) (Abduction: Consent: Oral Evidence) (Art 13(b))* are often referred to, and in particular, questions such as:

23 [2025] EWHC 2219 (Fam)

24 [2018] 2 FLR 74

25 2025] EWHC 114 (Fam)

26 [2024] EWHC 489 (Fam)

27 [2024] EWHC 3081 (Fam)

> '*the court needs to know what rights the mother and the children would have in Spain in order to address what risks night arise in the event of her returning there"* and "*without further information, I do not consider that [the risk of enforced separation] would necessarily be ameliorated by the mother being able to make a relocation application to the Spanish court*'

Conclusion of Chapter

1980 Hague Convention proceedings are technical and can be complex. There is a growing trend towards expert evidence on the issues relating to Article 13b and protective measures. Practitioners need to be alive to the issues to ensure proceedings are timetabled properly and all relevant issues are assessed, by experts when required.

CHAPTER FOUR

EXPERT EVIDENCE IN INHERENT JURISDICTION PROCEEDINGS

Inherent Jurisdiction

To consider it in a fairly modern context, Ward LJ in *Re* Z (A Minor) (Identification: Restrictions on Publication)[28] Ward LJ said:

> *'The wardship or inherent jurisdiction of the court to cast its cloak of protection over minors whose interests are at risk of harm is unlimited in theory though in practice the judges who exercise the jurisdiction have created classes of cases in which the court will not exercise its powers'*

In 2018, the then President of the Family Division, Sir James Munby, published official guidance on the jurisdiction of the family court titled: 'ALLOCATION OF CASES WITHIN THE FAMILY COURT TO HIGH COURT JUDGE LEVEL AND TRANSFER OF CASES FROM THE FAMILY COURT TO THE HIGH COURT'[29].

In the guidance, Sir James Munby set out the relationship between the family court and the High Court. He went on to state at paragraph 4:

> *'The High Court, of which the Family Division is part, is a superior court of record. It has unlimited jurisdiction. The*

[28] [1997] Fam 1, para 23

[29] https://www.judiciary.uk/wp-content/uploads/2018/02/pfd-guidance-2018-jurisdiction.pdf

> *family court, in contrast, is a creature of statute, with its jurisdiction defined by statute. The jurisdiction of the family court, although very extensive, is not unlimited'*

The key phrase in the guidance is that in respect of the '*unlimited jurisdiction*'. The guidance goes on to give various examples of cases, which must commence in the High Court. In the first part of the schedule at Part A, it states that '*family court does not have jurisdiction; must be commenced in the Family Division*'. They are:

> *'1 Inherent jurisdiction of the court relating to children (including applications for interim relief and injunctions invoking the inherent jurisdiction of the court and applications to make a child a ward of court or to bring such an order to an end)'*

The above is useful in illustrating the power of the inherent jurisdiction. In contrast to most of the family law proceedings which are heard in the Family Court, the High Court is in a unique position in that it can exercise and invoke the inherent jurisdiction.

<u>Wardship</u>

An interesting feature of High Court proceedings is the difference between the inherent jurisdiction and wardship. Both areas are dealt with in the High Court, but whilst they are at times linked, they must be separated as otherwise practitioners fall into a trap of seeking certain relief that is not necessary. It is a common misconception that the subject children have to be made wards in order for the court to exercise its inherent jurisdiction. This is not the case. The Family Procedure Rules ['FPR'] helpfully distil this myth and they distinguish the different characteristics of wardship. For example, the FPR 2010[30] defines[31] the distinguishing characteristics of wardship as follows:

> '(a) *custody of a child who is a ward is vested in the court; and*
>
> (b) *although day to day care and control of the ward is given to an individual or to a local authority, no important step can be taken in the child's life without the court's consent*'

In terms of a case law example, Parker J in AB v CD[32] stated the following:

> *Wardship is a way in which the 'inherent jurisdiction with regard to children' (ie the parens patriae jurisdiction) may be exercised. Once a child is a ward of court, that child is under the continuous protection of the court, even after a final order has been made determining the issues in respect of that child. Once a child is ward of court that child's place or country of residence or school cannot be changed without a court order*'.

A useful starting point is the authority of S (A Child) (Abduction: Hearing the Child)[33] and in particular paragraphs 12 – 16 which states:

> '*Proceedings concerning the welfare of a child whether in the Family Court or in the reserved jurisdictions of the High Court are subject to the same fundamental principles concerning effective access to justice for children who are the subjects of the applications that are made. There is no general rule in England and Wales that every child should be a party and that every child*

---

30 Practice Direction 12D, para 1.3

31 Ibid, para 1.3 (a) and (b)

32 [2014] 1 FLR 1439, para 51

33 [2014] EWCA Civ 1557

be represented by lawyers, by litigation friends or by welfare guardians. In each species of jurisdiction there are rules and practice directions that require or permit different forms of representation depending on the nature of the process and the facts of the case. There is often a delicate balance to be undertaken between the procedural protections that are afforded to a child by the process and the protection that may be necessary in respect of the impact on the child of the process (including the adversarial positions of the child's parents).

The underlying concept is that the child must be afforded effective access to justice so that the State does not infringe that child's article 6 and 8 ECHR rights. Without prejudice to the schemes that are in place for public and private law children applications under the Children Act 1989, this case is about the application of the general principles to proceedings in the inherent jurisdiction of the High Court. It should be recollected that in this case A was made a ward of court and was accordingly subject to the prerogative jurisdiction of the Crown otherwise known as the parens patriae jurisdiction, which is administered by the judges of the High Court.

There is a dispute between the parties about whether there are general principles that apply in a case of this kind. If there are, the key question that arises is whether the application of those general principles required something to be done that was not done on the facts of this case.

Article 12 of the United Nations Convention on the Rights of the Child 1989 [UNCRC] provides that:

> *"[1] States parties shall assure to the child who is capable of forming his or her own views the right to express those views freely in all matters affecting the child, the views of the child being given due weight in accordance with the age and maturity of the child.*

> *[2] For this purpose, the child shall in particular be provided the opportunity to be heard in any judicial and administrative proceedings affecting the child, either directly, or through a representative or an appropriate body, in a manner consistent with the procedural rules of national law."*

The UNCRC creates international obligations rather than domestic rights. That said, it is consistent with and has a persuasive interpretative effect on other international instruments that are binding on the United Kingdom. For example, article 24 of the Charter of Fundamental Rights of the European Union *provides that:*

> *"[1] Children shall have the right to such protection and care as is necessary for their well being. They may express their views freely. Such views shall be taken into consideration on matters which concern them in accordance with their age and maturity.*
>
> *[2] In all actions relating to children, whether taken by public authorities or private institutions, the child's best interests must be a primary consideration.'*

The Inherent Jurisdiction – General Principles

The key case is Re NY (A Child)[34]. This case outlined the principle that if a party is seeking a return order through the inherent jurisdiction, then the point of reference for the court is the subject child's welfare.

The Supreme court set out 8 principles. These 8 points are what practitioners need to have in mind for any inward or outward abduction case. Each principle will have an impact upon the timetable and therefore must be grappled with urgently. Inward and outward abduction

[34] [2019] UKSC 49

proceedings are 'summary' and therefore an applicant should ensure in particular, that the proceedings are timetabled and each of the below are considered:'

> *55. I respectfully suggest, however, that, before making a summary order under the inherent jurisdiction for this child to be returned to Israel, the Court of Appeal should have given (but did not give) at least some consideration to eight further, linked, questions.*
>
> *56. First, the court, which was sitting on 18 June 2019, should have considered whether the evidence before it was sufficiently up to date to enable it then to make the summary order. The mother's statement in answer to the claim under the Convention was dated 29 March 2019. In it she had devoted seven out of 67 paragraphs to assertions of the child's habitual residence in England and of particular circumstances said to demonstrate how happy and settled she had become. In his statement in reply dated 11 April the father had joined issue with the mother's assertions. The oral evidence given by the parties to the judge on 15 April had been limited to the issue of consent to the child's removal from Israel and so had not addressed these matters.*
>
> *57. Second, the court should have considered whether the judge had made, or whether it could make, findings sufficient to justify the summary order. The only relevant finding made by the judge had been that on 10 January 2019, only seven weeks after her arrival in England, the child had retained habitual residence in Israel. Was that sufficient to justify the making of a summary order five months later? In the light of the policy in favour of the making of substantive welfare determinations by the courts of habitual residence, did there need to be inquiry into the child's habitual residence at the relevant date, which, in the absence of an application, was in this case the date of the proposed order?*

58. Third, the court should have considered whether, in order sufficiently to identify what the child's welfare required for the purposes of a summary order, an inquiry should be conducted into any or all of the aspects of welfare specified in section 1(3) of the 1989 Act and, if so, how extensive that inquiry should be: see para 49 above. It might in particular have considered that the third of those aspects, namely "the likely effect on [the child] of any change in [her] circumstances", merited inquiry.

59. Fourth, the court should have considered whether in the light of Practice Direction 12J, an inquiry should be conducted into the disputed allegations made by the mother of domestic abuse and, if so, how extensive that inquiry should be: see para 50 above. The judge had made no findings about them. Instead, in accordance with the E case cited in para 12 above, he had, for the purposes of the claim under the Convention, made a reasonable assumption in relation to the maximum level of risk to the child arising out of any domestic abuse to be perpetrated by the father and had considered that such risk would be contained within acceptable limits by undertakings offered by the father, the enforceability of which in Israel the judge had not explored. Consideration should therefore have been given to whether, in a determination to be governed by the child's welfare, the judge's approach to the mother's allegations remained sufficient.

60. Fifth, the court should have considered whether, without identification in evidence of any arrangements for the child in Israel, in particular of where she and the mother would live, it would be appropriate to conclude that her welfare required her to return there.

61. Sixth, the court should have considered whether, in the light of its consideration of the five matters identified above, any oral evidence should be given by the parties and, if so, upon what aspects and to what extent.

62. Seventh, the court should have considered whether, in the light of its consideration of the same matters, a CAFCASS officer should be directed to prepare a report and, if so, upon what aspects and to what extent. It is noteworthy that in the L case discussed in para 43 above, a CAFCASS report had been prepared. It had been designed to ascertain the boy's wishes and feelings and so was apparently made as if pursuant to section 1(3)(a) of the 1989 Act: see para 14 of Baroness Hale's judgment. In her careful weighing, in paras 34 to 37 of her judgment, of the welfare considerations which militated both in favour of, and against, the boy's return to Texas, Baroness Hale relied to a significant extent upon the content of the CAFCASS report.

63. Eighth, the court should have considered whether it needed to compare the relative abilities of the Rabbinical Court in Jerusalem and the Family Court in London to reach a swift resolution of the substantive issues between the parents in relation to the child and to satisfy itself that the Rabbinical Court had power to authorise the mother to relocate with the child back to England: see para 34 above.

64. The effect of the above is not to submerge efficient exercise of the inherent jurisdiction to make a summary order within an ocean of onerous judicial obligations. The linked obligations are obligations only to consider the eight specified matters. There is no need for us to contemplate what the proper outcome of the Court of Appeal's consideration of them might have been. It is the fact that it failed even to consider them which yields the conclusion that it conducted no defensible analysis of the child's welfare prior to its determination to make the summary order and which led this court to uphold the mother's appeal'.

Accordingly, issues relating to PD12J, Cafcass, evidence generally relating to welfare is crucial. How these factors are considered can alter the timetable. If there needs to be a fact-finding, then this will create a delay. A welfare assessment is likely to be ordered only after a fact-finding hearing. Alternatively, if the matter only requires a welfare enquiry, then it should be noted that the paramountcy of the subject child's welfare may not necessarily require a full welfare enquiry. Each case is fact specific. Practitioners should have the 8 principles in consideration always during inherent jurisdiction cases particularly in cases relating to child abduction.

In addition to the above principles, it is important to differentiate between inward and outward abduction.

Inward Abduction

It is important practitioners are alive to two possibilities here:

A. The country where the children were abducted is a non-Hague state; or

B. The country where the children were abducted from, is a Hague state, but the inherent jurisdiction needs to be utilised.

In respect of point B, there are circumstances where the 1980 Hague Convention does not apply. For example, if the return is for a child over the aged of 16[35] and therefore the Convention does not apply. In these circumstances, the issue is that of welfare under the inherent jurisdiction. As outlined in *Re J (Child Returned Abroad: Convention Rights)*[36]

---

35 Re Q (Children) (1980 Hague Convention: Inherent Jurisdiction Summary Return) [2019] EWHC 490 (Fam) also see Article 4 of the 1980 Hague Convention

36 [2005] 2 FLR 802, at paragraph 25

> *'in all non-Convention cases, the courts have consistently held that they must act in accordance with the welfare of the individual child. If they do decide to return the child, that is because it is in his best interests to do so, not because the welfare principle has been superseded by some other consideration'*

Further, Re J makes clear there is a choice before the Court:

> *'it is plain, therefore, that there is always a choice to be made. Summary return should not be the automatic reaction to any and every unauthorised taking or keeping a child from his home country. On the other hand, summary return may very well be in the best interests of the individual child'*[37]

Moreover, as Baroness Hale stated in Re J, the following:

> *'The most one can say, in my view, is that the judge may find it convenient to start from the proposition that it is likely to be better for a child to return to his home country for any disputes about his future to be decided there. A case against his doing so has to be made. But the weight to be given to that proposition will vary enormously from case to case. What may be best for him in the long run may be different from what will be best for him in the short run. It should not be assumed, in this or any other case, that allowing a child to remain here while his future is decided here inevitably means that he will remain here for ever'*[38]

The above is a position. It is not a presumption and therefore depending upon the facts of a case, the issue can be grappled with.

---

37 Paragraph 28

38 Paragraph 32

Accordingly, an assessment is that of Children Act 1989 and welfare. In circumstances where there is clearly an international case in existence, there has been a vast amount of case law considering the issue. Therefore, points such as the connection the child have to each competing country[39] the child's views, the legal systems available in each country for example. There will be a broad assessment and in circumstances where a respondent seeks to defend a summary return application, they need to consider having a Cafcass assessment in respect of welfare. Welfare is the key concept and as described by Lord Donaldson MR in Re F (Minor) (Abduction: Jurisdiction)[40]*:*

> *'The welfare of the child is indeed the paramount consideration, but it has to be considered in two different contexts. The first is the context of which court shall decide what the child's best interests require. The second context, which only arises if it has first been decided that the welfare of the child requires that the English rather than a foreign court shall decide what are the requirements of the child, is what orders as to custody, care and control and so on, should be made.'*

Equally, in respect of any points relating to the legal system, there should be a consideration of a Part25 expert to address the issue (more on this below). The case of LM v DR[41] demonstrates the issue. The party resisting a summary return will have to demonstrate that the issue of the legal system in that country is relevant to the welfare of the child in circumstances where a return order is resisted.

Another consideration is the voice of the child. Just like 1980 Hague Convention cases, there is a vast number of reported decisions on the issue. Afterall, when the issue is that of welfare, the child's views are going

---

[39] Re L (Minors) (Wardship: Jurisdiction) [1974] 1 WLR 250

[40] [1991] 1 FLR 1

[41] [2016] EWHC 1943 (Fam)

to be a consideration within the checklist of factors and could ultimately, be a key one at that Practitioners should address this at the first case management hearing. Cafcass should be contacted in order to obtain their timescales to do a report as well as the remit of the report. As outlined earlier, a full welfare assessment may not be necessary and therefore the timing for the report to be completed may differ. The scope of the report should be addresses at the first hearing and recorded clearly in the report.

In terms of the essential nature of the child's voice, the Court of Appeal in Re S (A Child)[42] outlines the following international obligations:

> '[15] Article 12 of the United Nations Convention on the Rights of the Child 1989 [UNCRC] provides that:
>
> *'1. States parties shall assure to the child who is capable of forming his or her own views the right to express those views freely in all matters affecting the child, the views of the child being given due weight in accordance with the age and maturity of the child.*
>
> *2. For this purpose, the child shall in particular be provided the opportunity to be heard in any judicial and administrative proceedings affecting the child, either directly, or through a representative or an appropriate body, in a manner consistent with the procedural rules of national law."*
>
> *[16] The UNCRC creates international obligations rather than domestic rights. That said, it is consistent with and has a persuasive interpretative effect on other international instruments that are binding on the United Kingdom. For*

42 (Abduction: Hearing the Child) [2014] EWCA Civ 1557

example, art 24 of the Charter of Fundamental Rights of the European Union provides that:

"1. Children shall have the right to such protection and care as is necessary for their well being. They may express their views freely. Such views shall be taken into consideration on matters which concern them in accordance with their age and maturity.

2. In all actions relating to children, whether taken by public authorities or private institutions, the child's best interests must be a primary consideration.'

The 1980 Hague Convention would also not apply if the applicant cannot prove rights of custody immediately prior to the retention nor removal pursuant to Article 3[43].

Outward Abduction

Proceedings relating to outward abductions tend to be more difficult to progress and timetable and require practitioners to think strategically from the outset of proceedings. This is because, in circumstances where a respondent has abducted a child to a non-Hague state, then a number of practical obstacles arise and can materialise. Firstly, the action of the respondent to take a child to a non-Hague state within itself is a problem. The non-Hague state has no bilateral agreement with the Courts of England and Wales and therefore the respondent may be seeking to evade justice. Other issues that often arise in this case, which can involve children are:

A. Whether to go without notice or not;

43 Re W (Abduction: Father's Rights) [1998] 2 FLR 146

B. Any assistance that can be obtained from agencies / government bodies;

C. Tracing and locating the respondent / child;

D. Ensuring the respondent engages with the proceedings;

E. Enabling the child's voice to be heard; and

F. Ensuring compliance.

Expert Evidence – inherent jurisdiction

As a consequence of the above, the issues need to be determined first. Is it an inward or outward abduction and what is the level of risk. All these questions and focus is on the child's welfare. Then, the general trajectory of the case requires consideration in light of Re NY.

Typically, questions can arise as to:

- The necessity of protective measures; and
- The legal system in the other country.

Protective Measures

This has been dealt with in the previous chapter in relation to 1980 Hague Convention proceedings and Article 13b. In inherent jurisdiction proceedings, the necessity of protective measures and other protective features is very different. For example, a party may seek a return of a child to a country, but an issue may arise about whether the abducting parent can be afforded protective over there.

Given the inherent jurisdiction involves many countries, which are not signatories to the 1980 Hague Convention, an understanding of the legal system over there is likely to be necessary when it comes to protective measures.

An example of this at first instance is FB v KS[44] which concerned a summary return application to Philippines. As part of those proceedings, a single joint expert to provide an opinion on the relevant law in the Philippines was accounted for. As paragraph 29 outlined, the respondent argued '*legal rights to pursue applications in [the Philippines] are significantly prejudiced*' as a consequence of the contents of the expert report. This therefore required consideration by the trial judge. The assessment of the expert report had to be considered in light of the courts assessment of the parties. The judge dealt with the issue and commented as follows:

> *'While it is evident from the above that the system for determining disputes between parents about their children in the Philippines is not identical to that in this jurisdiction, in my judgment, it cannot be said that there is no effective relocation jurisdiction. KS would be able to pursue an application for custody, and although there are hurdles arising as a result of his status as an unmarried father which do not exist under the Children Act 1989, there is no absolute prohibition on a person in his position from obtaining custody and therefore being able to relocate with their child. The test of 'compelling reasons' is not an impossible threshold to reach, and I note that KS's own case is that FB is unfit to parent H because of the history of domestic abuse. That appears to be precisely the sort of compelling reason the courts in the Philippines would consider when forming a view as to whether the statutory presumption in favour of FB has been rebutted, having regard to H's welfare. The expert report is clear that KS's allegations of domestic abuse would be*

44 [2025] EWHC 827 (Fam)

> *taken into consideration under the holistic approach to best interests.*
>
> *It is submitted on behalf of KS that any orders or undertakings from FB in this jurisdiction would be worthless, as they could only be enforced here if H was present here (or was habitually resident here), and such enforcement would be required before the breach could be relied on in the courts of the Philippines.*
>
> *In my view, FB is likely to comply with orders or undertakings made in these proceedings. Although she has at times threatened in text messages that KS will never see H again, she has said in other messages and to the court in these proceedings that she wants H to have both her parents in her life and wishes to co-parent with KS. She has facilitated a relationship between her older child, G, and his father (albeit that KS says they did not have much contact with each other while he was living in the Philippines). FB understands that KS can bring proceedings in the Philippines and that any agreement reached, undertakings offered or orders made on the basis of her consent to them, would be put before the courts in that country, as would this judgment. FB has offered to give any undertaking or comply with any order the court considers appropriate'.*

There are also many other first instant decisions relating to the use of experts. There are a number of judgments on the use of experts in UAE. Many countries have fast developed and fast-paced legal jurisdictions, and each case is fact specific. In one case, one set of questions may be necessary and then in the other case, another set of questions will be relevant. Therefore, often even when dealing with the same countries, expert evidence may be required. Another example at first instance is H (A Child) (Refusal of Relocation to UAE)[45]. There was a Dubai expert

---

[45] [2025] EWHC 2691 (Fam)

in existence, but again context is important. In that case, it was apparent in the judgment that, at paragraph 1:

> *'H is five years and eight months old. She has been the subject of litigation nearly all her life. There have been so many orders and hearings in this jurisdiction and in Dubai, the parties are unable to agree how many have taken place. It appears there have been eighty two hearings and orders'.*

Therefore, history of litigation in Dubai was an issue. In many cases under the inherent jurisdiction, issues can arise as to:

- The voice of the child in the returning state;
- How litigation is conducted / timetabled (i.e, is there a relocation remedy);
- How can orders / undertakings be recognised and enforced;
- What is the availability of protections from the state, including social services and the government.

The issues can be vast and, again, fact specific.

<u>In Practice – Expert Evidence</u>

The first on-notice case management issue is key. It is likely this will be the hearing where proceedings are timetabled. Following Re NY, many issues may go hand in hand. For example, if PD12J is engaged and there is an element of a fact-finding, then of course, the issue of protection / recognition of protective orders and undertakings is likely to be an issue.

However, it is imperative that the relevant practitioner completes the necessary Part25 application. Identifying an expert is often likely to be the initial hurdle given unfamiliarity of other jurisdictions. It is however important that experts follow through with the Part25 criteria. Issue can arise, as it did before a judge in MB v KB & Ors[46], where for example it was commented in the judgment:

> *'the document provided in response to this letter of instruction is dated 20 November 2023. It is far from satisfactory. It does not address all of the questions posed in the letter of instruction and has reformulated a number of the other questions. The document also fails to comply with FPR Part 25 in a number of important ways:*
>
> *(1) The document does not identify its authors. It is stated as being provided b[the firm]; however, no detail is provided as to the individuals at the firm who prepared the report.*
>
> *(2) The document does not identify the expert's qualifications and experience.*
>
> *(3) It lacks the statement required by PD25B para 9.1(i) as to the expert's duties; and*
>
> *(4) It lacks the appropriate statement of truth'*

<u>Conclusion of Chapter</u>

This chapter has outlined the complexity in respect of inherent jurisdiction proceedings. Several different issues can arise whether it is outward or inward child abduction. Notwithstanding this, it is clear that Re NY provides a useful framework for practitioners and the court to work with. This case requires consideration in every case to ascertain if expert evidence is going to be necessary and if so on what issue.

[46] [2023] EWHC 3177 (Fam)

CHAPTER FIVE

EXPERT EVIDENCE IN PUBLIC LAW PROCEEDINGS

Introduction

This Chapter will focus on the key issues that often arise in public law proceedings when it comes to expert evidence.

As emphasised in Re B (A Child) Care Proceedings: Threshold Criteria)[47], the House of Lords made it clear of the 'stringent and demanding' tests required in care proceedings. Baroness Hale said it is 'necessary to explore and attempt alternative solutions' (paragraph 198). Lord Neuberger said that 'before making an adoption order in such a case the court must be satisfied that there is no practical way of the authorities (or others) providing the requisite assistance and support' (paragraph 105). In public law proceedings, where the state is involved – Article 6 and Article 8 rights are engaged to the highest level.

In Re Z (A Child: Independent Social Work Assessment)[48] HHJ Bellamy sitting as a High Court Judge stated:

> *'In any case in which a local authority applies to the court for a care order, the assessment of the parent is of critical importance. That assessment will be a key piece of the evidential jigsaw, which informs the local authority's decision-making, in particular with respect to the formulation of its care plan. If the assessment is deficient then it is likely to undermine the*

47 (2013) UKSC 33

48 (2014) EWHC 729

> *reliability of the decision-making process. It follows from there, that any assessment of a parent must be, and must be seen to be, fair, robust and thorough'* (paragraph 130).

The Rules

The FPR 2010 and CFA 2014 require full consideration whenever an expert is considered in public law proceedings. Types of expert assessments include mental health diagnoses, cognitive assessments, substance misuse evaluations, medical opinions, and culturally specific assessments. For parenting assessment, independent social workers can also be utilised.

Part 25 of the Family Procedure Rules 2010 provides the statutory rules of procedure governing the use of expert witnesses in children proceedings under s.13 of the 2014 Act.

Part 25.43 of the FPR states:

> *'The court may give permission as mentioned in paragraph (2) only if the court is of the opinion that the expert evidence is necessary to assist the court to resolve the proceedings.'*

The meaning of "necessary" in this context was considered in Re HL (A child)[49], where the Court said:

> *'The short answer is that 'necessary' means necessary. It is, after all, an ordinary English word. It is a familiar expression nowadays in family law, not least because of the central role it plays, for example, in Article 8 of the European Convention and the wider Strasbourg jurisprudence. If elaboration is required, what precisely does it mean? That was a question considered, albeit in a rather different context, in Re P (Placement Orders:*

---

[49] [2013] EWCA Civ 655

> *Parental Consent) [2008] EWCA Civ 535, [2008] 2 FLR 625, paras [120], [125]. This court said it "has a meaning lying somewhere between 'indispensable' on the one hand and 'useful', 'reasonable' or 'desirable' on the other hand", having "the connotation of the imperative, what is demanded rather than what is merely optional or reasonable or desirable." In my judgment, that is the meaning, the connotation, the word 'necessary' has in rule 25.1.'*

In addition to the FPR, Section 13 of the 2014 Act controls the use of expert evidence in children proceedings (as defined in FPR r.25.2(1)). Section 13 of the 2014 Act provides:

> *'13 Control of expert evidence, and of assessments, in children proceedings*
>
> *(1) A person may not without the permission of the court instruct a person to provide expert evidence for use in children proceedings.*
>
> *(2) Where in contravention of subsection (1) a person is instructed to provide expert evidence, evidence resulting from the instructions is inadmissible in children proceedings unless the court rules that it is admissible.*
>
> *(3) A person may not without the permission of the court cause a child to be medically or psychiatrically examined or otherwise assessed for the purposes of the provision of expert evidence in children proceedings.*
>
> *(4) Where in contravention of subsection (3) a child is medically or psychiatrically examined or otherwise assessed, evidence resulting from the examination or other assessment is inadmissible in children proceedings unless the court rules that it is admissible.*

(5) In children proceedings, a person may not without the permission of the court put expert evidence (in any form) before the court.

(6) The court may give permission as mentioned in subsection (1), (3) or (5) only if the court is of the opinion that the expert evidence is necessary to assist the court to resolve the proceedings justly.

(7) When deciding whether to give permission as mentioned in subsection (1), (3) or (5) the court is to have regard in particular to—

(a) any impact which giving permission would be likely to have on the welfare of the children concerned, including in the case of permission as mentioned in subsection (3) any impact which any examination or other assessment would be likely to have on the welfare of the child who would be examined or otherwise assessed,

(b) the issues to which the expert evidence would relate,

(c) the questions which the court would require the expert to answer,

(d) what other expert evidence is available (whether obtained before or after the start of proceedings),

(e) whether evidence could be given by another person on the matters on which the expert would give evidence,

(f) the impact which giving permission would be likely to have on the timetable for, and duration and conduct of, the proceedings,

(g) the cost of the expert evidence, and

(h) any matters prescribed by Family Procedure Rules'

Accordingly, where the court grants an application made pursuant to FPR r.25(6) for permission to instruct a person to provide expert evidence for use in children proceedings under s.13(1) of the 2014 Act, then the court will give directions specifying the date by which the expert will provide a written report and specifying the date by which the expert is to receive the letter of instruction pursuant to FPR r.25.8(b).

Accordingly, in light of the above. Timing is a key issue.

Timing – Principles

Practitioners should refer to the FPR 2010, and in particular PD12A. This provision outlines the purpose of each hearing in public law proceedings. The starting point is 'Case Management Hearings'. As the name suggests, the purpose of such hearings is to timetable the proceedings. Taken directly from the rules:

Stage 2 – Case Management Hearing	
Advocates' Meeting (including any litigants in person)	**Case Management Hearing**
No later than 2 business days before CMH (or FCMH if it is necessary)	CMH : Not before day 12 and not later than day 18 A FCMH is to be held only if necessary, it is to be listed as soon as possible and in any event no later than day 25
• Consider information on the Application Form and Annex documents, the LA Case Summary, and the Case Analysis	• Court gives detailed case management directions, including:

Stage 2 – Case Management Hearing	
• Identify the parties' positions to be recited in the draft Case Management Order • Identify the parties' positions about jurisdiction, in particular arising out of any international element • **If necessary, identify proposed experts and draft questions in accordance with Part 25 and the Experts Practice Directions** • Identify any disclosure that in the advocates' views is necessary • Immediately notify the court of the need for a contested ICO hearing and any issue about allocation • LA advocate to file a draft Case Management Order in prescribed form with court by 11a.m. on the business day before the CMH and/or FCMH	— Considering jurisdiction in a case with an international element; — Confirming allocation — Drawing up the timetable for the child and the timetable for the proceedings and considering if an extension is necessary — Identifying additional parties, intervenors and representation (including confirming that Cafcass/CAFCASS CYMRU have allocated a Children's Guardian and that a litigation friend is appointed for any protected party or non-subject child) — Giving directions for the determination of any disputed issue about litigation capacity — Identifying the key issues — Identifying the evidence necessary to enable the court to resolve the key issues — Deciding whether there is a real issue about threshold to be resolved — Determining any application made under Part 25 and otherwise ensuring compliance

Stage 2 – Case Management Hearing	
	with Part 25 where it is necessary for expert(s) to be instructed — Identifying any necessary disclosure and if appropriate giving directions — Giving directions for any concurrent or proposed placement order proceedings — Ensuring compliance with the court's directions — If a FCMH is necessary, directing an advocates' meeting and Case Analysis if required — Directing filing of any threshold agreement, final evidence and Care Plan and responses to those documents for the IRH — Directing a Case Analysis for the IRH — Directing an advocates' meeting for the IRH — Listing (any FCMH) IRH, Final Hearing (including early Final Hearing) — Giving directions for special measures and/or interpreters and intermediaries — Issuing the Case Management Order

Accordingly, applications for expert evidence needs to be made at such a hearing. FPR, PD12A, rule 5.1 outlines in terms of timing for proceedings in public law cases:

> *'5.1*
>
> *5.1 The timetable for the proceedings –*
>
> *(1) The court will draw up a timetable for the proceedings with a view to disposing of the application –*
>
> *(a) without delay; and*
>
> *(b) in any event within 26 weeks beginning with the day on which the application was issued in accordance with section 32(1)(a)(ii) of the Children Act 1989.'*

Section 32(5) Children Act 1989 further stipulates:

> *'Period within which application for order under this Part must be disposed of.*
>
> *(1) A court in which an application for an order under this Part is proceeding] shall (in the light of any provision in rules of court that is of the kind mentioned in subsection (2)(a) or (b))]—*
>
> *(a) draw up a timetable with a view to disposing of the application—*
>
> *(i) without delay, and*
>
> *(ii) in any event within twenty-six weeks beginning with the day on which the application was issued; and]*

> *(b) give such directions as it considers appropriate for the purpose of ensuring, so far as is reasonably practicable, that that timetable is adhered to.*
>
> *(2) Rules of court may—*
>
> *(a) specify periods within which specified steps must be taken in relation to such proceedings; and*
>
> *(b) make other provision with respect to such proceedings for the purpose of ensuring, so far as is reasonably practicable, that they are disposed of without delay'.*

In November 2022, the President of the Family Division published, 'Local Practice Note: Ensuring adherence to the Public Law Outline in London'. Within that, the following:

> *'It is now clear to me that there is a need for a radical resetting of the culture within the Family Court so that the system reconnects with the strictures of the PLO and, once again, aims to meet the statutory requirement of completing each public law case within 26 weeks'*

The document was useful in many ways, in that headings and points emphasised within it focused on making every hearing matter, the need for all to ensure compliance with directions but also in terms of witness evidence, the following was stated:

> *'Controlling expert evidence*
>
> *25. The strict test for whether the court requires expert evidence to determine proceedings is clear and well established.*
>
> *26. The court will only permit the instruction of an expert where it is* demonstrated *to the court that to do so is* necessary *to assist*

the court to resolve the proceedings justly' and not simply that it is merely desirable or helpful.

27. The fact that all parties agree that a particular expert is necessary will not *automatically lead to permission being given for that expert to be instructed. The question of whether expert evidence is* necessary *is a matter for the court.*

28. FPR 2010 r.25.9(2) stipulates that the court will not direct the attendance of the expert at a final hearing unless it is necessary *to do so in the interests of justice. It is incumbent on any party seeking to cross-examine an expert to make an application for the court to direct the attendance of the expert'.*

Expert Evidence – Public Law Proceedings

The necessity of what type of expert is required in public law proceedings varies case by case. As the President outlined in TG (A Child)[50], paragraph 31 outlined:

'Whether applying the present test or the new test, the case management judge will have to have regard to all the circumstances of the particular case. The judge will need to consider the nature of the particular expert evidence the admission of which is in issue. The evidence of an expert in one discipline may be of marginal use; the evidence of an expert in another discipline may be crucial. The judge will also need to be sensitive to the forensic context. The argument for an expert in a care case where permanent removal is threatened may be significantly stronger than in a case where the stakes are not so high. We strive to avoid miscarriages of justice, but human justice is inevitably fallible and case management judges need to be alert to the risks. The Oldham and Webster cases stand as

---

50 [2013] EWCA Civ 5

> *terrible warning to everyone involved in the family justice system, the latter as stark illustration of the fact that a miscarriage of justice which comes to light only after the child has been adopted will very probably be irremediable: see W v Oldham Metropolitan Borough Council [2005] EWCA Civ 1247, [2006] 1 FLR 543, Oldham Metropolitan Borough Council v GW & PW [2007] EWHC 136 (Fam), [2007] 2 FLR 597, and Webster v Norfolk County Council and the Children (By Their Children's Guardian) [2009] EWCA Civ 59, [2009] 1 FLR 1378. But although the case management judge must be alert to the risks, the potential for such tragedies does not entitle a parent in care proceedings to an expert for the asking: see Re S; WSP v Hull City Council [2006] EWCA Civ 981, [2007] 1 FLR 90, paras [15]-[18]. Nor does it relieve the case management judge of the duty to exercise his or her discretion in accordance with the various provisions of the Family Procedure Rules to which I have drawn attention'.*

Further, at paragraph 32, when considering case management decisions for expert evidence, the following was outlined:

> *'in every care case, as indeed in every case, the case management judge will need to assess and evaluate the degree of likelihood that a particular expert's evidence, or the evidence of an expert in a particular discipline, will or will not be of assistance to the parties in exploring, and to the judge in determining, the issues to which the evidence in question is proposed to be directed. It is vital that the case management judge keeps an open mind when deciding whether or not to permit expert evidence. The judge will need to be alert to the risks posed by what may turn out to be 'bad science'. On the other hand, the judge must always be alert to the possibility that some forensically unfamiliar or even novel expert discipline may provide the key to explaining what at first blush appears to be a familiar type of case: consider, for example, what happened in Webster v Norfolk County Council*

and the Children (By Their Children's Guardian) [2009] EWCA Civ 59, [2009] 1 FLR 1378.'

Assessments

Section 13(3) and (4) of the CFA 2014 provides as follows:

> *'(3) A person may not without the permission of the court cause a child to be medically or psychiatrically examined or otherwise assessed for the purposes of the provision of expert evidence in children proceedings.*
>
> *(4) Where in contravention of subsection (3) a child is medically or psychiatrically examined or otherwise assessed, evidence resulting from the examination or other assessment is inadmissible in children proceedings unless the court rules that it is admissible'.*

Where an interim care/supervision order is made, ChA 1989, s 38(6) enables the court to give a direction for 'medical, psychiatric or other examination' of a child but only where the court considers this 'necessary' to assist the court in dealing with the case (s 38(7A)). This was considered In Re G (Interim Care Order: Residential Assessment)[51], by Lady Hale but also Re C (A Minor) (Interim Care Order: Residential Assessment)[52] where it was stated:

> *'Next, it is true that s 38(6) and (7) only refer to the assessment 'of the child' and not, as is proposed in the present case, a joint assessment of the child and the parents, including the parents' attitude and behaviour towards the child. But it is impossible to assess a young child divorced from his environment. The interaction between the child and his parents or other persons*

[51] [2005] UKHL 68

[52] [1997] AC 489

> *looking after him is an essential element in making any assessment of the child. This is shown particularly clearly by cases in which the courts have to decide whether the threshold requirements of s 31 are satisfied because of the harm to the child that is likely to be suffered because the child is beyond parental control. How can the court determine that issue without considering the relationship between the child and the parents? The court has no power to order the parents to take part in any assessment against their wishes, any more than, as the final words of s 38(6) show, the court can order the child to do so if the child is capable of making an informed decision. But what the interests of justice require is not a power to compel the parent to take part in such assessment but a power in the court to override the powers over the child which the local authority would otherwise enjoy under the interim care order. If the narrower construction were to be adopted the local authority could simply refuse to allow the child to take part in any assessment with his parents'.*

In terms of constructing the provisions, the following was outlined:

> *'In my judgment, therefore, s 38(6) and (7) of the Act are to be broadly construed. They confer jurisdiction on the court to order or prohibit any assessment which involves the participation of the child and is directed to providing the court with the material which, in the view of the court, is required to enable it to reach a proper decision at the final hearing of the application for a full care order. In exercising its discretion whether to order any particular examination or assessment, the court will take into account the cost of the proposed assessment and the fact that local authorities' resources are notoriously limited'.*

As such, Section 38(6) of the Act permits the court, when making an interim care or supervision order to 'give such directions (if any) as it considers appropriate with regard to the medical or psychiatric examination or other assessment of the child'.

The matter was further considered In Re T (Residential Parenting Assessment)[53] by the Court of Appeal. The court outlined it was within the judge's discretion to refuse permission for an assessment of a parent. The court outlined:

> *'The present case is one in which the judge examined carefully, with evidence, whether the proposed assessment would contribute information that she needed and concluded, for carefully articulated reasons, that it would not because it could only gather evidence about the mother's capacity in the limited sphere of a residential placement and because even if that assessment was positive, that would not overcome the mother's difficulty that the therapeutic work that she required to put herself in a position to care for her child would take longer than the period for which the child could wait for a permanent home. Before taking this decision, the judge enabled the mother to obtain evidence addressing the future prognosis by permitting her to instruct the psychiatrist and the psychologist and she arranged for the hearing of 21 March at which their evidence could be heard and challenged.*
>
> *I appreciate the constraints of a hearing for the purposes of determining whether to make a direction under s 38(6); such a hearing is inevitably shorter and focused more narrowly than a full hearing at which the threshold criteria are considered and/or a final welfare decision is taken and it will often leave more unanswered questions than such a hearing. The judge must, of course, take that limitation into account in determining whether the proposed assessment is necessary. I would not wish anything that I say here to be interpreted so as to start a practice of*

---

53 [2011] EWCA Civ 812

> *extended s 38(6) hearings which are indistinguishable from the final hearing. It is a matter for the individual judge to regulate the nature and extent of the material upon which the s 38(6) decision is taken and the format of the s 38(6) hearing, and this aspect of the judge's case management will, like most case management, be highly dependent on the facts of the individual case'.*

On this issue, Lady Hale in Re G (Interim Care order: Residential Assessment)[54] commented:

> *'[71] ... it will always be necessary to think early and clearly about what assessments are indeed necessary to decide the case. In many cases, the local authority should be able to make its own core assessment and the child's guardian to make an independent assessment in the interests of the child. Further or other assessments should only be commissioned if they can bring something important to the case which neither the local authority nor the guardian is able to bring. No one denies that this was a particularly complex and difficult case in which expert psychological assessment of the risks was essential. But that is not always so'.*

Psychiatric / Psychological Evidence

In care proceedings, the use of a psychologist / psychiatrist may be regarded as necessary. This will again depend on the facts of the case and the issues and whether it is relevant to the issue of threshold.

The High Court considered the issue of psychological assessments in West Northamptonshire Council v The Mother (Psychological

---

[54] [2005] UKHL 68

Assessments)[55]. By way of important facts from this case, the judgment outlines:

> *'I note that there is nothing in the interim Threshold or the Social Work Evidence Template ("SWET") which suggest that the Mother suffers from cognitive impairment or significant communication difficulties. There is no reference to her having a Special Educational Needs Statement or having attended anything other than a mainstream school'.*

The judge then proceeded outline the part25 application and the information contained within that. The judge outlined:

> *'It hardly needs stating that these three matters are exceedingly common in care proceedings, and do not begin without further detail, to justify a psychological assessment. An application under Part 25 for a psychological/cognitive assessment must be accompanied by proper evidence which explains why the case goes beyond the standard difficulties faced by many parents in care proceedings. The evidence must explain why the parent's needs cannot be properly managed by careful use of language and the professionals taking the time to explain matters in an appropriate manner. The evidence must address why such an assessment is necessary rather than just something that would be "nice to have".*
>
> *It would often be the case that if one parent does have cognitive issues this will have been identified at school, during previous interactions with the Local Authority and/or in pre-proceedings work. These earlier interventions will frequently identify whether there are cognitive challenges, and how they can best be handled'.*

55 [2024] EWHC 395 (Fam)

The judge considered the application and submissions. The judge outlined:

> 23. *'This application does not come close to meeting the test of being "necessary" to resolve the proceedings, and in my view should never have been made. The fact that Mr Leach referred to taking a "belt and braces" approach indicates strongly that the proper test was not being considered either by counsel when she advised or by the solicitors when they made the application. Unfortunately, such misconceived applications are exceedingly common, particularly in respect of applications for psychologists to undertake cognitive assessments.*
>
> 24. *Such applications waste considerable resources, both in the courts, but also in the local authorities and Cafcass when they lead to unnecessary hearings and unnecessary expense. It is important that they are not granted without the Court properly addressing the correct test.*
>
> 25. ...
>
> 26. *A test of necessity does not mean that a report would be "nice to have" or might help in determining what psychological support the parent might need in the future. That is not necessary to resolve the proceedings'*

Medical Evidence

A significant part of public law proceedings is threshold. At times, non accidental injury cases can be relevant. Medical evidence in these cases are important. As Dame Elizabeth Butler-Sloss P in re U (A Child)

(Department for Education and Skills intervening) and in Re B (A Child) (Department for Education and Skills intervening)[56] at paragraph23:

> *'The judge in care proceedings must never forget that today's medical certainty may be discarded by the next generation of experts or that scientific research will throw light into corners that are at present dark'.*

Further, at paragraph 10, Hedley J said in Re R (Care Proceedings: Causation)[57]:

I have been impressed over the years by the willingness of the best paediatricians and those who practise in the specialities of paediatric medicine to recognise how much we do not know about the growth patterns and what goes wrong in them, particularly in infants. Since they grow at a remarkable speed and cannot themselves give any clue as to what is happening inside them, and since research using control samples is self-evidently impossible in many areas, perhaps we should not be surprised. In my judgment, a conclusion of unknown aetiology in respect of an infant represents neither professional nor forensic failure. It simply recognises that we still have much to learn and it also recognises that it is dangerous and wrong to infer non-accidental injury merely from the absence of any other understood mechanism. Maybe it simply represents a general acknowledgement that we are fearfully and wonderfully made.'

In short, medical cases in public law disputes can be wide-ranging. There can be a whole host of issues relating to the case a local authority seeks to pursue. In these circumstances, as Dame Elizabeth Butler-Sloss P in Re T[58] at paragraph 33:

---

56 [2004] EWCA Civ 567

57 [2011] EWHC 1715 (Fam)

58 [2004] EWCA Civ 558

> *'Evidence cannot be evaluated and assessed in separate compartments. A judge in these difficult cases must have regard to the relevance of each piece of evidence to other evidence and to exercise an overview of the totality of the evidence in order to come to the conclusion whether the case put forward by the local authority has been made out to the appropriate standard of proof.'*

Further, as per Peter Jackson LJ in Re R (Children: Findings of Fact)[59] at paragraph 34:

> *'...It is wrong to describe the medical evidence as the canvas against which the other evidence was to be considered. Medical and non-medical evidence are both vital contributors in their own ways to these decisions and neither of them has precedence over the other.'*

<u>The Attendance of Experts</u>

There has been a lot of debate about the attendance of experts. In short, whether and how they can or should be challenged. The principles were considered by Mr Justice MacDonald in A Local Authority v X (Attendance of Experts)[60]. After having considered all the authorities concerning expert evidence, particularly in the public law context, his lordship outlined guidance at paragraph 58:

> *'Drawing these threads together, it is possible to divine some general principles that will be applicable in each case a court is required to decide under FPR r.25.9(2) whether it is necessary in the interests of justice to direct the attendance of the expert:*

---

59 2024] EWCA Civ 153

60 (Rev1) [2025] EWFC 137

i) The general rule is that expert evidence is to be given in writing pursuant to FPR 2010 r. 25.9(1). This is not simply a requirement for the expert to provide their report in writing, but the general rule as to how evidence will be given at the hearing by an expert in family proceedings, including proceedings under Part IV of the Children Act 1989. Namely, in writing rather than orally unless the test of necessity in the interests of justice is met.

ii) In the first instance the appropriate way of interrogating the written expert evidence is in writing pursuant to FPR 2010 r. 25.10. With the court's permission, and where appropriate and consistent with the Overriding Objective, questions in writing may extend beyond simply clarification of the expert report.

iii) Where appropriate, the court may also direct discussion between the experts pursuant to FPR 2010 r.25.16 to define and refine areas of agreement and disagreement between the experts.

iv) It is to be anticipated that, in a proportion of cases, the process for written questions under FPR 2010 r.25.10 and discussion between the experts under FPR 2010 r. 25.16 will render it unnecessary to direct the attendance of the expert at the final hearing.

v) Pursuant to the terms of FPR r.25.9(2), the attendance of the expert at the final hearing will only be directed where it is necessary to do so in the interests of justice.

vi) Where a party seeks the attendance of the expert at the hearing, following the putting of any written questions and any experts meeting that party should make an application for a direction to that effect by way of Form C2, setting out the reasons why it is said that such attendance is necessary in the interests of justice.

vii) In determining whether it is necessary in the interests of justice to direct the attendance of the expert, an intense focus on the content of the expert evidence by reference to the issues before the court, undertaken in the context of the Overriding Objective in FPR Part 1, the provisions of FPR Part 25, the importance in certain cases of the role of challenging evidence in ensuring the overall fairness of the hearing and the nature and extent of the task of the court in assessing the evidence before it, will determine necessity in the interests of justice, rather than general considerations of the nature of the proceedings, the seriousness and potential consequences of those proceedings or the rights engaged therein per se. The fact that all parties agree that the expert should attend the hearing will not be determinative.

viii) In applying the test of necessity in the interests of justice, questions likely to be at the forefront of the court's mind are (a) the extent to which the expert evidence is relied on, (b) the extent to which the expert evidence is disputed, (c) whether the parts of the expert evidence that are disputed are central to determination of the issues the court must decide, (d) the degree of consensus or disagreement between the instructed experts, (e) whether it is possible fairly to deal with the points of dispute in writing without the attendance of the expert, (f) whether the expert evidence deals with a particularly novel or controversial area or an area where there is a lack of scientific consensus or rapidly evolving research, (g) whether expert evidence suggests that a dogmatic approach has been taken by an expert or that the reputation or amour propre of the expert is at stake, (h) what other evidence is available to the court relevant to determining the issues before it, (i) the position of the party against whom allegations are made and (j) whether the opportunity to challenge the expert evidence is necessary to ensure the overall fairness of the hearing. This is not an exhaustive list.

> *ix) Where attendance and cross examination is permitted, the expert should be given advance notice of the topics (not the questions) to be covered and of any fresh evidence.*
>
> *x) Where the court does permit the attendance for cross examination of an expert the court may impose a strict time limit for cross-examination and specify the topics to be dealt with.'*

Other Assessments

There can in public law proceedings be other assessments. Such as, an independent social work report in circumstances where a parenting assessment is sought or there's a challenge to an existing parenting assessment. Ordinarily, as it is the case of the local authority, they will embark upon parenting assessment. But again, every case is fact specific and a local authority may not seek to assess someone. This also relates to viability assessments and other assessments such as special guardianship assessments. Whilst the local authority have, often, the ability to embark upon such assessments in-house or to outsource them, there can be occasions in which a independent social worker assessment is sought by a party or an interested party in proceedings.

The case of H-W (Children)[61] made clear that a decision leading to adoption requires the rigorous evaluation and comparison of all the realistic possibilities for a child's future in the light of the Court's factual findings.

This court's case of Re UDTQ (No Adequate Care Planning)[62]: stated

> *160. 'The Social Worker told the Court her view, "I do not want to deny ['D'] having a forever family and having that*

---

61 [2022] UKSC 17

62 [2024] EWFC 19

opportunity," "the children should have the opportunity to be adopted and have a forever family," and "the Local Authority does not want to deny the children the opportunity of being matched with potential adopters." It appeared to this Court that the Local Authority's approach was to consider adoption as a starting point. That is the wrong approach.

161. Regrettably, in this Court's experience, it appears there is a regular misunderstanding or misapplication of the words of Lady Hale in Re B [2013] UKSC 33; [2013] 2 FLR 1075. At paragraph 198 of the judgment of the Supreme Court, Lady Hale held:

> *"...it is quite clear that the test for severing the relationship between parent and child is very strict: only in exceptional circumstances and where motivated by overriding requirements pertaining to the child's welfare, in short, where nothing else will do."*

162. It appears to this Court that the shorthand phrase 'nothing else will do' regularly becomes detached from the rest of Lady Hale's words and misinterpreted out of context by many to mean, 'adoption is the gold standard and anything less is not good enough.'

The court must exercise care that it does not fall into the difficulty (or endorse the local authority falling into the problem) noted by Lady Hale in Re B: "*it cannot be said that 'nothing else will do' when nothing else has been tried*" (paragraph 223).

Conclusion of Chapter

Public law proceedings are perhaps the area where there is a lot of focus on expert evidence from the outset. The role of experts has a very important role to play when a party wishes to challenge evidence, including that which goes directly towards threshold. Most parties are legally aided in public law proceedings and therefore expert costings, as well as timescales are always key issues to consider in public law proceedings.

CHAPTER SIX

EXPERT EVIDENCE IN PRIVATE LAW PROCEEDINGS

Introduction to Chapter

Private law disputes are those proceedings where there is a dispute as to the use of parental responsibility or any other conflict in respect of the upbringing of the child which requires the courts determination. Proceedings can be varied in terms of complexity and the issues that the court is required to consider. At times, proceedings can escalate where the proceedings may turn into public law proceedings or there are fact-finding hearings. Private law disputes are commenced and heard in the Family Court but can be allocated to either Lay Justices, District Judges or Circuit Judges. In certain circumstances, cases can be reallocated to the High Court in cases of particular complexity.

Proceedings concerning children in the private law context is governed by the Children Act 1989. The ambit is stipulated by Section 1 (1) which states:

> *'(1) When a court determines any question with respect to—*
>
> *(a) the upbringing of a child; or*
>
> *(b) the administration of a child's property or the application of any income arising from it,*
>
> *the child's welfare shall be the court's paramount consideration.*
>
> *(2) In any proceedings in which any question with respect to the upbringing of a child arises, the court shall have regard to the general principle that any delay in determining the question is*

likely to prejudice the welfare of the child. The statute then refers to the 'welfare checklist'. It goes on to record:

'(3) In the circumstances mentioned in subsection (4), a court shall have regard in particular to—

(a) the ascertainable wishes and feelings of the child concerned (considered in the light of his age and understanding);

(b) his physical, emotional and educational needs;

(c) the likely effect on him of any change in his circumstances;

(d) his age, sex, background and any characteristics of his which the court considers relevant;

(e) any harm which he has suffered or is at risk of suffering;

(f) how capable each of his parents, and any other person in relation to whom the court considers the question to be relevant, is of meeting his needs;

(g) the range of powers available to the court under this Act in the proceedings in question.

(4) The circumstances are that—

(a) the court is considering whether to make, vary or discharge a section 8 order, and the making, variation or discharge of the order is opposed by any party to the proceedings; or

(b) the court is considering whether to make, vary or discharge a special guardianship order or an order under Part IV.

(5) Where a court is considering whether or not to make one or more orders under this Act with respect to a child, it shall not

make the order or any of the orders unless it considers that doing so would be better for the child than making no order at all.'

In the private law context, there are other provisions relating to the Children Act 1989 on topics such as parental responsibility, who can apply for orders and other provisions. However, as for the purposes of considering children participation, the welfare checklist is an important starting point.

Applying the Welfare Checklist

As can be seen from the welfare checklist above, there is a series of factors the court must consider when concerned with a dispute. Ultimately, it is the court who is considering the checklist and applying it to the facts of a case, and this is an important consideration that people need to be aware off working in this field, it is the court's application and decision. However, the court often is required to be assisted in their decision-making process.

In the run up to the Children Act 1989, the Law Commission[63] proposed the checklist and set out the aims of the provision:

'Perhaps most important of all, we are told that such a list could assist both parents and children in endeavouring to understand how judicial decisions are made. At present, there is a tendency for advisers and clients (and possibly even courts) to rely on "rules of thumb" as to what the court is likely to think best in any given circumstances. A checklist would make it clear to all what, as a minimum would be considered by the court.'

However, given there are many different factors within the checklist, the question of weight to be attached to each one has been subject to case law

63 Family Law Review of Child Law: Guardianship and Custody (1988) Law Com No 172

debate. Ultimately, 'each case turns on its own facts and the weight to be given to various factors will change from case to case'[64].

Welfare Reports and Expert Reports

The first step to consider welfare in proceedings is often the Section 7 report. When proceedings commence via a c100, the process enters into a gatekeeping stage. From this moment, Cafcass will be tasked to embark upon safeguarding checks. The remit and purpose of safeguarding letters appears in PD12B, Rule 13.1 onwards which states: '

> *13.1*
>
> *Where an application is made for a child arrangements order (but not necessarily for specific issue or prohibited steps orders), before the FHDRA (see paragraph 14 below) Cafcass / CAFCASS Cymru shall identify any safety issues by the steps outlined below.*
>
> *13.2*
>
> *Such steps shall be confined to matters of safety. The Cafcass Officer or (in Wales) the Welsh Family Proceedings Officer (WFPO) shall not discuss with either party before the FHDRA any matter other than one which relates to safety. The parties will not be invited to talk about other issues, for example relating to the substance of applications or replies or about issues concerning matters of welfare or the prospects of resolution. If such issues are raised by either party, they will be advised that such matters will be deferred to the FHDRA when there is equality between the parties and full discussion can take place*

---

64 *Re W (Children) (Relocation: Removal Outside the Jurisdiction)* [2011] EWCA Civ 345 per Wall P at [117].

which will be a time when any safety issues that have been identified can also be taken into account.

13.3

In order to inform the court of possible risks of harm to the child Cafcass / CAFCASS Cymru will carry out safeguarding enquiries. For all child arrangements orders this will include seeking information from local authorities, and carrying out police checks on the parties. For all other applications received from the court on the form C100, Cafcass / CAFCASS Cymru will carry out a screening process and will undertake those checks if in the professional judgment of the Cafcass officer, or the WFPO in Wales, such checks are necessary.

13.4

Cafcass / CAFCASS Cymru will, if possible, undertake telephone risk identification interviews with the parties and if risks of harm are identified, may invite parties to meet separately with the Cafcass Officer, or WFPO in Wales, before the FHDRA to clarify any safety issue.

13.5

Cafcass / CAFCASS Cymru shall record and outline any safety issues for the court, in the form of a Safeguarding letter (in Wales, this is called a 'Safeguarding report').

13.6

The Cafcass officer, or WFPO, will not initiate contact with the child prior to the FHDRA. If contacted by a child, discussions relating to the issues in the case will be postponed to the day of the hearing or after when the Cafcass officer or WFPO will have more knowledge of the issues.

13.7

Within 17 working days of receipt by Cafcass / CAFCASS Cymru of the application, and at least 3 working days before the hearing, the Cafcass Officer or WFPO shall report to the court, in a Safeguarding letter / report, the outcome of the risk identification work which has been undertaken. The letter / report should specify which court forms filed by the parties (C100, C7 and C1A) have been considered.

13.8

Further, Cafcass and CAFCASS Cymru are required, under section 16A Children Act 1989, to undertake (and to provide to the court) risk assessments where an officer of the Service ('Cafcass Officer' or WFPO) suspects that a child is at risk of harm'

The safeguarding letter is essential in cases involving risk and domestic abuse. However, the safeguarding letter highlights other important information:

- Police involvement;
- Previous local authority involvement; and
- Recommendations for the case, including case management.

The above is important because it may be apparent that there are historic social work involvement relating to a family. If so, then a social work local authority may be better placed to deal with the case than perhaps Cafcass.

Ultimately, the first piece of advice to look out for in the safeguarding letter is whether a Section 7 is recommended and if so, on what remit and what timescales. The Section 7 report will go through the welfare checklist and be an intensive piece of work where the reporting officer will provide the court with recommendations at the Dispute Resolution Appointment hearing ['DRA'] in the hope parties can settle the case.

The Section 7 report is also the gateway to consider further involvement in respect of children. A child subject to the report has the opportunity through the report to provide their wishes and feelings and the reporting officer will consider their welfare when providing recommendations. However, the Section 7 report may also provide other direct ways to involve children. Typically, they may involve:

- A letter to the court written by the children which goes towards the wishes and feelings aspect of the welfare checklist; and / or

- A recommendation that a guardian should be appointed and the reasons for outlining why.

The child subject to the report can prepare a letter, which is often attached to or incorporated in the report and such a letter is under their wishes and feelings category. Alternatively, the officer may recommend that the child is joined to proceedings / have a guardian appointed for them when that applies.

It is worth noting that it does not only have to be Cafcass who is to do a Section 7 report. The benefit of course with Cafcass is that if a guardian is appointed, it would be somebody from Cafcass and they have their own internal systems in place and procedures. However, as outlined earlier there can be cases where there have been previous or existing social work involvement. In these circumstances, Cafcass will, and it will have to be Cafcass given they are the only ones that can do the safeguarding letter, recommend from the outset in the safeguarding letter that the local authority is likely to be best placed to embark upon the Section 7 report. This could be not only due to the existing or past local authority involvement, but also the child subject to the proceedings may be part of a child in need or child protection plan and ultimately, there may be an allocated social worker in existence. Another option is an independent social worker to complete a Section 7 report which is sometimes an option where reports are sought much quicker. For example, in relocation cases where there may be an element of urgency or if the parties are able to afford an expert, it is likely an independent social worker can prepare a report much quicker, sometimes 6 – 8 weeks, or even less, in comparison to some areas where Cafcass can take in excess to 16

As a consequence of the issues relating to timescales, a party may seek to appoint an Independent Social Worker. This will need to be made through a formal part25 application. Pursuant to FPR PD 3.10(f), it is important in any application to address '*why the expert evidence proposed cannot properly be given by a Cafcass officer or the local authority (social services undertaking a core assessment) or any other party to the proceedings or an expert already instructed in the proceedings*'. Arguments can include:

A. An ISW report is likely to be more thorough and comprehensive (for example, more meetings, scope for interim reports, more contact being observed)

B. An ISW report is likely to be quicker;

C. Cafcass has indicated that there is no further role for Cafcass, but this is a case in which a comprehensive section 7 report will be required; and

D. There is no assurance of social worker continuity with a local authority section 7 report.

Expert Evidence and Section 7 reports

Under s.7 Children Act 1989, when considering any question relating to a child under the Act the court may order a report "*on such matters relating to the welfare of that child as are required to be dealt with*" [s.7(1)

Children Act 1989]. This chapter seeks to outline the aims of such a report, the circumstances in which it would be ordered, who is best placed to write it and key considerations for practitioners and parents alike.

<u>What is a section 7 report?</u>

A section 7 report is a type of report that the court can order when it needs more information about a child's welfare. The author will gather information from a variety of sources, including external agencies (such as the police, the NHS and schools), conversations with parents/guardians and direct work with the child to provide the court with recommendations about what is in the child's best interests. The ability of the court to order such a report is set out at section 7 of the Children Act 1989:

> *"Welfare reports.*
>
> *(1) A court considering any question with respect to a child under this Act may—*
>
> *(a) ask [F1an officer of the Service] [F2or a Welsh family proceedings officer]; or*
>
> *(b) ask a local authority to arrange for*
>
> *(i) an officer of the authority; or*
>
> *(ii) such other person (other than [F1an officer of the Service] [F2or a Welsh family proceedings officer]) as the authority considers appropriate,*
>
> *to report to the court on such matters relating to the welfare of that child as are required to be dealt with in the report."*

Section 7(3) CA 1989 allows for the report to "be made in writing, or orally, as the court requires." In practice, the report will almost always be made in writing, but the author is usually summoned to give evidence on their report at a contested final hearing.

Section 7 reports can encompass a wide range of issues and when ordering the report, the court will specify the precise areas which the author of the s 7 report should analyse and consider in the order. These can include:

Where and with whom the child should live

- Where the child should spend time with the parent they do not live with, and for how long
- The child's wishes and feelings (depending on their age and understanding)
- All aspects of the child's welfare, including their physical, emotional and educational needs and whether they are being met and by whom
- Whether the child has suffered or is at risk of suffering harm
- The parenting capacity of one or both parents with regard to any allegations raised or findings that have been made
- The effects of any proposed change of circumstances on the child, for example changes to where and with whom they live, or changes to their personal identity, such as their name or religious upbringing
- Whether a Local Authority should be requested to undertake a report under section 37 of the Children Act 1989, to investigate the need for care/supervision order applications or which services or assistance the child and their family may require

- Recommendations for arrangements for the child, including contact, change of residence, change of educational provision etc

In essence, the report's purpose is to provide the court with updated information from an expert on the child's welfare, to help the court to make decisions. This wide ambit gives the court the discretion to choose what issues need to be addressed.

As the report will often contain third-party evidence, i.e from conversations with teachers or the police, section 7(4) CA 1989 is a very broad provision which enables the court to disregard all rules of evidence and to take into account any statement or evidence which is relevant to the question in issue.

Who writes the section 7 report?

When determining whether it should be Cafcass or the local authority who should be the author of such a report, the court should consider the current level of involvement of the local authority in the family. The revised policy[65] between Cafcass and the Association of Children's Services (dated November 2022) stipulates that the Local Authority should be the author of the s 7 report if one of the following circumstances as specified below applies. Without that specified involvement of the local authority then Cafcass are the appropriate authors. These circumstances are:

(a) A child is the subject of an open and active statutory social work case with the Local Authority;

65 https://proceduresonline.com/trixcms2/media/23543/cafcass-adcs-s7-letter-and-policy-11112022.pdf

(b) In the last 12 weeks before the section 7 is ordered there has been a statutory social work assessment of a child's welfare in accordance with s.17 or s.47 of the Children Act 1989;

(c) In the last 12 weeks before the section 7 is ordered the child has been subject to a child in need plan or a child protection plan.

Pursuant to Rule 12.75 of the Family Procedures Rules 2010, regardless of which agency prepares the report, each agency is obliged to assist the other and to provide the other agency with all relevant information. Notably, the revised policy does not compromise the fact that the ultimate decision lies with the court, meaning that even in the event of the existence of one of the above factors, the court can still order a Cafcass officer author the report nonetheless.

Cafcass Officer

The most common section 7 author is a Cafcass officer.

Cafcass stands for "Children and Family Court Advisory and Support Service," an organisation formed of Cafcass officers who are often experienced social workers. Their role is to provide independent advice and support to help the family court and families make decisions in the best interests of children. They are an integral aspect of most public and private children law proceedings, specifically in cases where welfare concerns have been identified.

Private law proceedings most commonly begin with one party with parental responsibility applying to the court for a Child Arrangements Order, through issuing a C100 application form. Within the form, there is a box which can be ticked in order to alert the court that there has been previous Local Authority involvement and therefore indicating whether there may be welfare concerns which need to be address in the proceedings.

Typically, around 17 days before the First Hearing and Dispute Resolution Appointment ("FHDRA") Cafcass will complete safeguarding checks. They will use information from public agencies, including the police, to very briefly analyse and identify any possible welfare concerns for the children, both historic and current. They will compile this information into a letter which will be before the court at the FHDRA.

Alongside identifying any risks, the letter will contain recommendations for the court on how they should proceed at this stage. These can include recommendations on interim contact arrangements, i.e contact between the FHDRA and the next hearing, whether a section 7 report should be ordered, whether a fact-finding hearing will be necessary and whether the parents should undergo any co-parenting courses during proceedings. Cafcass may also attend the FHDRA to speak to the parties and will provide confirmation of their safeguarding checks and be available to the court during the course of the hearing.

The author of a section 7 report could be subject to scrutiny and cross examination at the final hearing if one party does not agree with the analysis/recommendations. The court may therefore consider that due to their level of court experience and familiarity with giving oral evidence, a Cafcass officer may be best played to provide this information to the court[66].

Local Authority Social worker

As per the revised policy, if there has been recent involvement or is current involvement from the Local Authority, i.e if the family is "known to them," they may be best placed to undertake the report. They are typically able to complete such a report in a timely manner due to their easy access to the information they hold on the family, which would prevent delay and therefore not prejudice the child. Further, allocated or

---

66 Waite LJ in *Re W (Welfare Reports)* [1995] 2 FLR 142 [§146]

recently allocated social workers will likely be more familiar and able to deal with the relevant issues which caused the proceedings to reach the doors of the court in the private law context.

Independent Social Worker

In limited circumstances, it may be appropriate for an independent social worker ("ISW") to undertake the section 7 report. Notably however, the Family Justice Review Final Report recommends that independent social workers should only be used "exceptionally" (paras 3.131, 3.132).

The decision to instruct an ISW can include both strategic and practical considerations. These can include where:

- The Family Court did not deem a s7 report necessary, but a parent is sensitive that their child's needs/welfare should be assessed before the court determines any issues;

- The family is well known to the Local Authority – it may be felt by one or both of the parties that a neutral, uninfluenced professional is required to provide the assessment, relative to the social workers who are familiar with the parents and may be influenced in their recommendations.

- A faster resolution of proceedings is preferred – ISWs will typically have quicker time limits in which they are able to conduct and conclude their report.

To instruct an ISW, the parties will either have to agree to the instruction, or one party will have to issue a Part 25 Application. Typically, this application is made before the first hearing and, akin to whether a s7 report is required, will be determined by the Family Court at the first hearing. To successfully apply to instruct an ISW the Family Court must deem the report necessary – i.e would the court be able to make an order relating to the caring arrangements of this child without the ISW's report.

Such a decision will typically mean parties meeting the costs of the report themselves, which can lead to disagreement which may require the court to resolve. This issue may be sidestepped by one parent agreeing to cover the costs of the ISW, or by agreeing to split the costs in a certain way.

"<u>such other person as the authority considers appropriate</u>"

Section 7(1)(b)(ii) confers on the Local Authority discretion as to the other person appointed, and the court has no power to control that appointment or to require the Local Authority to pay for expert advice. The court has been clear that it is not appropriate to use s.7(1)(b)(ii) to make an order requiring the Local Authority to appoint an officer to obtain a report from a child psychiatrist (*Re K (Contact: Psychiatric Report)*[67]).

<u>When would a section 7 report be ordered?</u>

The court will typically direct a section 7 report to be undertaken at one of three stages of proceedings: (i) at the FHDRA, following the Cafcass safeguarding letter, (ii) at a directions hearing where a fact-finding hearing has been determined as necessary and proportionate (although rarely at this stage), or (iii) after a fact-finding hearing.

The timing of the report may also be determined by the engagement of PD 12J. The following provisions within PD 12J are relevant when considering a s 7 report:

> *'[21] In <u>any case where a risk of harm to a child resulting from domestic abuse is raised as an issue</u>, the court should consider directing that a report on the question of contact, or any other*

[67] [1995] 2 FLR 432, CA

matters relating to the welfare of the child, be prepared under s 7 of the Children Act 1989 by an Officer of Cafcass or a Welsh family proceedings officer (or local authority officer if appropriate), unless the court is satisfied that it is not necessary to do so in order to safeguard the child's interests.

[22] If the court directs that there shall be a fact-finding hearing on the issue of domestic abuse, the court will not usually request a s 7 report until after that hearing. In that event, the court should direct that any judgment is provided to Cafcass/CAFCASS Cymru; if there is no transcribed judgment, an agreed list of findings should be provided, as set out at paragraph 29.

[23] Any request for a s 7 report should set out clearly the matters the court considers need to be addressed.'

In practice, under PD 12J copies of all applications for child arrangements orders are sent to Cafcass to enable them to undertake initial screening of the parties, including seeking information from the police about any previous convictions and information from the Local Authority about any previous referrals concerning them. Before the first hearing, Cafcass notifies the court of the results of their searches and will make recommendations as to who should author the s.7 report, and when it should commence.

What happens after the report is written?

Any party who does not agree with the report's recommendations may challenge these at a final hearing, including by putting questions to the author and making submissions to the court about why they disagree with the recommendations. It is open to the parties to ask the court to order an addendum to the section 7 report if this is required. This is typically used to clarify a particular area within the report which may be unclear, to address a new, pressing situation or event which has occurred since the previous report which may invalidate the previous recommendations, or to provide a short update on the circumstances of the family if significant time has passed since the report was submitted. Again, if this report was completed by an ISW, the parties will be expected to fund such an addendum and the court will need to be satisfied to the necessity

Whilst the decision of the court is ultimately one for the court alone to make, the section 7 report must be taken into account when evaluating that decision as made clear in Re P (Custody of Children: Split Custody Order)[68] [] with the court having to give reasons in circumstances where they deviate from the report's recommendations as further cemented in Re J (Children) (Residence: Expert Evidence)[69].

Key Considerations

For parents/guardians, it is imperative that they engage openly and honestly with the section 7 author, most significantly by remaining child-focused. It is very clear to authors of the report when a child has been influenced or "told what to say" by a parent before they commence direct work with the author. Therefore, as much as possible, parents must refrain from seeking to influence or involve the children in any conversations about the proceedings, and must never tell the child what to say to the section 7 author.

For practitioners, the decision to seek a section 7 report is often not a decision which is theirs to make. Rather, in practice such reports are routine and even mandated in certain cases (such as those which invoke PD 12J). The questions for practitioners are therefore not if a section 7 report is required, but when to suggest one is directed (especially where there is to be a fact-finding hearing) and submissions who should author

68 [1991] 1 FLR 337, CA

69 [2001] 2 FCR 44, CA

the report, what issues specifically should be addressed and who should bear the costs (if an ISW).

Section 7 reports remain central to private law children proceedings, to aid the court in making decisions as to a child's welfare by essentially providing a window into their lived experiences, which can then be used to make decisions in their best interests.

Expert Evidence – Implacable Hostility

In private law proceedings, there is often the phrase 'parental alienation' utilised. This is a complex term and there is a debate about it. However, for the purposes of this book, there can be expert evidence in situations where implacable hostility arises. Some ISW's or experts also utilise the term 'alienating' behaviours. On this label, the President in Re C ('Parental alienation'; Instruction of Expert)[70] commented:

> *'It is not the purpose of this judgment to go further into the topic of alienation. Most Family judges have, for some time, regarded the label of 'parental alienation', and the suggestion that there may be a diagnosable syndrome of that name, as being unhelpful. What is important, as with domestic abuse, is the particular behaviour that is found to have taken place within the individual family before the court, and the impact that that behaviour may have had on the relationship of a child with either or both of his/her parents. In this regard, the identification of 'alienating behaviour' should be the court's focus, rather than any quest to determine whether the label 'parental alienation' can be applied'*

In Re B (A Child)[71] the following was stated:

[70] [2023] EWHC 345 Fam

[71] [2016] EWCA Civ 1088

> *'Implacable hostility is exactly that: a case where one parent has become (usually irrationally and for poor motives) implacable opposed to contact taking place between a child and his or her absent parent. That is ... or may be very different from a case where a child has been alienated from a parent.'*

In Re D (Intractable Contact Dispute: Publicity)[72] the early identification for the court to resolve any issues of such a nature was emphasised:

> *'The court should grasp the nettle ... allegations should be speedily investigated and resolved, not left to fester unresolved and a continuing source of friction and dispute. Court time must be found — and found without delay —for fact finding hearings. Judges must resist the temptation to delay the evil day in the hope that perhaps the problem will go away.'*

In private law proceedings PD12J requires full consideration. It is flagged up out the outset in the sense it forms part of the safeguarding enquiries. Concepts of alienation and domestic abuse require serious consideration because from the Court of Appeal in Re H-N and Others[73], it is imperative to have early identification of the issues[74].

Most frequently psychiatric or psychological assessment of a party and/or subject child(ren) can become an issue in the case. In Re A and B (Parental Alienation: No. 1)[75] the court relied upon the evidence of a number of experts. A psychiatrist, psychologist and psychotherapist. Such evidence was decisive in providing an insight into the children's presentation, mental health and emotional development and behaviours,

---

72 [2004] EWHC 727 (Fam)

73 [2021] EWCA Civ 448

74 Also see PD12J, paragraphs 5, 16 and 17.

75 [2020] EWHC 3366 (Fam)

including how these differed between the children. In addition, these experts were able to comment upon the potential consequences for the children in the long-term if the status quo were to continue and provide an insight into the family dynamics generally and the alienating parent's motivation to change. Further, these experts were crucial in providing recommendations to the court in respect of how to progress the children's relationship with their father. There are also other first instance cases outlining similar issues, such as Re T (Parental Alienation)[76]. However, practitioners should also note a recent case of Mrs Justice Judd on the issue of expert evidence in the case of O v C[77] which in particular considered the approach of reopening findings.

One of the leading authorities and guidance is now found in the judgment of Re C ('Parental alienation'; Instruction of Expert)[78]. This judgement, from the President provides an overview on expert evidence. A further relevant and useful decision is found in a first instance decision in Re GB (Part 25 Application: Parental Alienation)[79]. The grounds of appeal before the Circuit Judge was (as outlined at paragraph 8):

> *'(i) The Judge was wrong to order a psychological assessment, which invites the expert to determine the factual matrix of disputed allegations, contrary to the President's decision in Re C (Parental Alienation: Instruction of Expert) [2023] EWHC 345 (Fam);*
>
> *(ii) The Judge was wrong to order a psychological assessment of the parents and the children without considering the test of*

76 [2019] EWHC 3854 (Fam)

77 [2025] EWFC 334

78 [2023] EWHC 345 Fam

79 [2023] EWFC 150

necessity under Part 25 of the Family Procedure Rules 2010; and

(iii) The judge failed to give any reasons for ordering a psychological assessment'The following passage from the judgment sets out why the appeal was permitted:'

26. The application for expert evidence was an important application in this long running case. It required careful and anxious scrutiny. This experienced Judge was aware of the dispute between the parties on the issue of the instruction of the expert. He plainly had Part 25 of the Family Procedure Rules in mind, having referred to the relevant rule in the course of the hearing.

27. This appellate Court has the benefit of transcript of whole hearing in Court below. It was identified by Counsel for the Children's Guardian at that hearing that the main issue for determination was around the Guardian's application for permission to instruct an expert. The lower court heard submissions from all parties. The Children's Guardian, supported by the father, asserted that expert evidence was necessary. The mother raised a series of concerns. She did not agree that expert evidence was necessary. She made clear written submissions setting out her objections, querying the necessity of the instruction, elaborated upon further in oral submissions, including her concern that the children have already been exposed to series of professionals and that further exposure would be harmful.

28. There was a plain dispute between the parties on the question of whether a further expert should be appointed. There was further dispute between the parties as to the questions the expert should be directed to address. They were the issues which the lower Court was equipped to resolve. It was the Judge's role to adjudicate upon those issues.

29. It must be assumed that the Judge rejected each of the mother's submissions. It is widely recognised that Judges sitting in the Family Court, where the intense and unabating pressure of work is very great and resources limited, face enormous difficulties and challenges. Regrettably, with respect to this experienced Judge, no judgment was given by the lower Court in any form. The Judge did not engage in the arguments raised by the parties. No reasons were given by the Judge at all, addressing the test of necessity, in circumstances where information already before the Court below included existing expert evidence. No facts had been found by the Court on the disputed issue of parental alienation. There was no consideration by the Judge of the mother's assertion that the father had not completed the work recommended by the previous expert Dr Lopez. There was no consideration by Judge of the potential harm to the children of exposing them to another professional, where they had already been required to meet the Guardian and a Local Authority Social Worker. I reject the submission that the Judge's reasons can be implied or read holistically. There was, very regrettably, no determination by the lower Court of the key issue in dispute, namely, whether expert evidence was necessary, by reference to the relevant factors in section 13(7) of the 2014 Act. The omission of a judgment is significant. That was not simply a procedural error. Judgments are the means through which Judges address the litigants and the public at large and explain their reasons for reaching their conclusions. A judgment providing reasons for rejecting one party's submissions or preferring the submissions of another party was a fundamental aspect of the Court's duty to deal with the case justly.

30. In the judgement of this Court, each of the grounds of appeal are plainly made out. This Court must conclude that in reaching his decision to permit further expert evidence, this experienced Judge did not engage with the issues in dispute, did not adjudicate on the disputed issue by reference to the relevant legal principles and did not provide the parties with any reasons for granting the application. In this Court's judgement, the decision of the lower Court was wrong and must be set aside'.

Identity of Expert

Henke J in the High Court presided over an appeal in Re: A (A Child: Appeal: Case Management Decision: Identity of Expert)[80]. There were three grounds, but the issue of expert assessment was one. Reference was made to a previous appeal in Re N (A Child) (Instruction of Expert)[81]. In Re N, Baker J when dealing with the issue about the instruction for an expert, commented:

> '*In these circumstances it is not necessary to say whether it could ever be right to specify an expert of a particular gender. I do not, however, rule out the possibility that such an order could be justified. As ever, all will depend on the circumstances. Justice requires the court to adopt a procedure which pays due respect to persons whose rights are significantly affected by its decisions.*'

In the case management appeal before Henke J, her ladyship considered the evidence, the litigation history, grounds of appeal and arguments put forward and determined:

> '*On the facts of this case, I consider that the Appellant has put forward good reason why a female psychologist should be used. Again, on the facts of this case, I consider that the best possible assessment evidence will be obtained by appointing a female psychologist to undertake the assessment. Thus, the Article 6 rights of both parties will be observed. In particular, the Appellant, who is a victim of third-party male violence, will*

80 [2024] EWHC 1669 (Fam)

81 [2022] EWCA Civ 1588

> *have the best opportunity to participate in the assessment process and give of her best during the assessment. The appointment of a female psychologist is most likely to engage this Appellant in the assessment process. It would also limit the opportunity for any further objection to the assessment and thus any further delay'*

Conclusion of Chapter

As this chapter has outlined, the use of expert evidence in private law proceedings can be varied. The main focus nonetheless remains the welfare of the child/children to the proceedings. Private law proceedings do not have the same limitations regarding delay as public law proceedings, but delay is nonetheless prejudicial to the welfare of a child/children. As such, an application for expert evidence must be focused and timetabled in an effective manner.

MORE BOOKS BY LAW BRIEF PUBLISHING

‘The Electronic Communications Code: A Practical Guide – Second Edition’ by Kerry Bretherton KC, James Castle, Mark Loveday
‘A Practical Guide to the Independent School Standards – September 2023 Edition’ by Sarah McKimm
'A Practical Guide to Estate Administration and Crypto Assets' by Richard Marshall
‘A Practical Guide to Parental Alienation in Private and Public Law Children Cases’ by Sam King QC & Frankie Shama
‘Contested Heritage – Removing Art from Land and Historic Buildings’ by Richard Harwood QC, Catherine Dobson, David Sawtell
‘The Limits of Separate Legal Personality: When Those Running a Company Can Be Held Personally Liable for Losses Caused to Third Parties Outside of the Company’ by Dr Mike Wilkinson
‘A Practical Guide to Transgender Law’ by Robin Moira White & Nicola Newbegin
‘A Practical Guide to ‘Stranded Spouses’ in Family Law’ by Mani Singh Basi
‘A Practical Guide to Residential Freehold Conveyancing’ by Lorraine Richardson
‘A Practical Guide to Pensions on Divorce for Lawyers’ by Bryan Scant
‘A Practical Guide to Challenging Sham Marriage Allegations in Immigration Law’ by Priya Solanki
‘A Practical Guide to Digital Communications Evidence in Criminal Law’ by Sam Willis
‘A Practical Guide to Legal Rights in Scotland’ by Sarah-Jane Macdonald
‘A Practical Guide to New Build Conveyancing’ by Paul Sams & Rebecca East
‘A Practical Guide to Inherited Wealth on Divorce’ by Hayley Trim
‘A Practical Guide to Practice Direction 12J and Domestic Abuse in Private Law Children Proceedings’ by Rebecca Cross & Malvika Jaganmohan
‘A Practical Guide to Confiscation and Restraint’ by Narita Bahra QC, John Carl Townsend, David Winch
‘A Practical Guide to the Law of Forests in Scotland’ by Philip Buchan
‘A Practical Guide to Health and Medical Cases in Immigration Law’ by Rebecca Chapman & Miranda Butler
‘A Practical Guide to Bad Character Evidence for Criminal Practitioners by Aparna Rao
‘A Practical Guide to Extradition Law post-Brexit’ by Myles Grandison et al
‘A Practical Guide to Hoarding and Mental Health for Housing Lawyers’ by Rachel Coyle

'Stephens on Contractual Indemnities' by Richard Stephens
'A Practical Guide to the EU Succession Regulation' by Richard Frimston
'A Practical Guide to Solicitor and Client Costs – Second Edition' by Robin Dunne
'Constructive Dismissal – Practice Pointers and Principles' by Benjimin Burgher
'A Practical Guide to Religion and Belief Discrimination Claims in the Workplace' by Kashif Ali
'A Practical Guide to the Law of Medical Treatment Decisions' by Ben Troke
'Fundamental Dishonesty and QOCS in Personal Injury Proceedings: Law and Practice' by Jake Rowley
'A Practical Guide to the Law in Relation to School Exclusions' by Charlotte Hadfield & Alice de Coverley
'A Practical Guide to Divorce for the Silver Separators' by Karin Walker
'The Right to be Forgotten – The Law and Practical Issues' by Melissa Stock
'A Practical Guide to Planning Law and Rights of Way in National Parks, the Broads and AONBs' by James Maurici QC, James Neill et al
'A Practical Guide to Election Law' by Tom Tabori
'A Practical Guide to the Law in Relation to Surrogacy' by Andrew Powell
'A Practical Guide to Claims Arising from Fatal Accidents – Second Edition' by James Patience
'A Practical Guide to Asbestos Claims' by Jonathan Owen & Gareth McAloon
'A Practical Guide to Stamp Duty Land Tax in England and Northern Ireland' by Suzanne O'Hara
'A Practical Guide to the Law of Farming Partnerships' by Philip Whitcomb
'A Practical Guide to the Law of Unlawful Eviction and Harassment – Second Edition' by Stephanie Lovegrove
'A Practical Guide to Costs in Personal Injury Claims – Second Edition' by Matthew Hoe
'A Practical Guide to the General Data Protection Regulation (GDPR) – Second Edition' by Keith Markham
'A Practical Guide to Working with Litigants in Person and McKenzie Friends in Family Cases' by Stuart Barlow
'Protecting Unregistered Brands: A Practical Guide to the Law of Passing Off' by Lorna Brazell
'A Practical Guide to Secondary Liability and Joint Enterprise Post-Jogee' by Joanne Cecil & James Mehigan

'A Practical Guide to the Pre-Action RTA Claims Protocol for Personal Injury Lawyers' by Antonia Ford
'A Practical Guide to Neighbour Disputes and the Law' by Alexander Walsh
'A Practical Guide to Coercive Control for Legal Practitioners and Victims' by Rachel Horman
'A Practical Guide to the Law of Driverless Cars – Second Edition'
by Alex Glassbrook, Emma Northey & Scarlett Milligan
'A Practical Guide to TOLATA Claims' by Greg Williams
'A Practical Guide to Elderly Law – Second Edition' by Justin Patten
'A Practical Guide to Responding to Housing Disrepair and Unfitness Claims' by Iain Wightwick
'A Practical Guide to the Law of Bullying and Harassment in the Workplace' by Philip Hyland
'How to Be a Freelance Solicitor: A Practical Guide to the SRA-Regulated Freelance Solicitor Model' by Paul Bennett
'A Practical Guide to Prison Injury Claims' by Malcolm Johnson
'A Practical Guide to Advising Clients at the Police Station' by Colin Stephen McKeown-Beaumont
'A Practical Guide to Antisocial Behaviour Injunctions – Second Edition' by Iain Wightwick
'Practical Mediation: A Guide for Mediators, Advocates, Advisers, Lawyers, and Students in Civil, Commercial, Business, Property, Workplace, and Employment Cases' by Jonathan Dingle with John Sephton
'The Mini-Pupillage Workbook' by David Boyle
'A Practical Guide to Crofting Law' by Brian Inkster
'A Practical Guide to the Law of Domain Names and Cybersquatting' by Andrew Clemson
'A Practical Guide to the Law of Gender Pay Gap Reporting' by Harini Iyengar
'NHS Whistleblowing and the Law' by Joseph England
'Employment Law and the Gig Economy' by Nigel Mackay & Annie Powell
'A Practical Guide to Noise Induced Hearing Loss (NIHL) Claims' by Andrew Mckie, Ian Skeate, Gareth McAloon
'An Introduction to Beauty Negligence Claims – A Practical Guide for the Personal Injury Practitioner' by Greg Almond
'Intercompany Agreements for Transfer Pricing Compliance' by Paul Sutton
'Zen and the Art of Mediation' by Martin Plowman
'A Practical Guide to Adoption for Family Lawyers' by Graham Pegg

'A Practical Guide to Industrial Disease Claims' by Andrew Mckie & Ian Skeate
'A Practical Guide to Conducting a Sheriff Court Proof' by Andrew Stevenson
'A Practical Guide to Vicarious Liability' by Mariel Irvine
'A Practical Guide to Applications for Landlord's Consent and Variation of Leases' by Mark Shelton
'A Practical Guide to Relief from Sanctions Post-Mitchell and Denton' by Peter Causton
'A Practical Guide to Equity Release for Advisors' by Paul Sams
'A Practical Guide to Financial Services Claims' by Chris Hegarty
'A Practical Guide to Financial Ombudsman Service Claims' by Adam Temple & Robert Scrivenor
'A Practical Guide to Running Housing Disrepair and Cavity Wall Claims – Second Edition' by Andrew Mckie & Ian Skeate
'A Practical Guide to Holiday Sickness Claims – Second Edition' by Andrew Mckie & Ian Skeate
'Arguments and Tactics for Personal Injury and Clinical Negligence Claims' by Dorian Williams
'A Practical Guide to Drone Law' by Rufus Ballaster, Andrew Firman, Eleanor Clot
'On Experts: CPR35 for Lawyers and Experts' by David Boyle
'An Introduction to Personal Injury Law' by David Boyle

These books and more are available to order online direct from the publisher at www.lawbriefpublishing.com, where you can also read free sample chapters. For any queries, call us on 0844 587 2383 or email us at mail@lawbriefpublishing.com.

Our books are all generally in stock at www.amazon.co.uk with free next day delivery for Prime members, and at good legal bookshops such as Wildy & Sons.

We are regularly launching new books in our series of practical day-to-day practitioners' guides. Visit our website and join our free newsletter to be kept informed and to receive special offers, free chapters, etc.

You can also follow us on Twitter at www.twitter.com/lawbriefpub.

www.ingramcontent.com/pod-product-compliance
Ingram Content Group UK Ltd.
Pitfield, Milton Keynes, MK11 3LW, UK
UKHW020148290926
15471UKWH00004B/755

9 781918 241150